FASCINATING WEXFOR

Des Kiely

Fascinating Wexford History

VOLUME TWO

Another fascinating collection of County Wexford

historical events, spanning twelve centuries.

A heady brew for lovers of Irish history.

DES KIELY

PARSIVAL PRESS

Published by the Parsifal Press, Newry

A CIP record for this title is available from The British Library

ISBN: 978-0-9933960-8-3

The author has made every reasonable effort to contact the copyright
holders of photographs and texts reproduced in this book.
The publisher apologizes for any errors or omissions and would be
grateful if notified of any corrections that should be incorporated
in future reprints or editions of this book.

Special thanks to Katherine Carroll, Eileen Cloney, Michael Dempsey,
Alice Hunt, David M. Kiely, Nadia Michnik, Michael Murphy,
Tom and Teresa Wickham.

Photo credits: Wesley Almeida, Michael Brazzill, Father Francis Browne,
Cork Examiner, Paddy Donovan, Dreamworks Pictures, Ireland from the
Skies, Irish Examiner, Irish Heritage Trust, Irish National Heritage Park,
John Ironside, Nadia Michnik, National Library of Ireland,
National Portrait Gallery London, Ros Tapestry, Michael Snoek.

Cover art and design by the author
Set in 10.5 Iowan Old Style by the author

Printed by Printrun Ltd, Dublin

As always, to Mel, Michelle, Kathy, Simon and Lucy

ABOUT THE AUTHOR

Des Kiely is by profession a graphic designer living in Wexford. He can trace his family history back to the village of Stradbally in County Waterford and to the house where his great-great-great grandfather John Kiely was born in 1778. The  family moved north to Derry and again back south to Dublin, then Wicklow, so Des has almost completed the journey back home to Waterford. His hobbies include photography, art, music and writing local history. This is his third book on Wexford history, the first two being his bestsellers *Famous Wexford People in History* and *Fascinating Wexford History, Volume One*.

CONTENTS

INTRODUCTION

'If you don't know history,' wrote the novelist Michael Crichton, 'then you don't know anything. You are a leaf that doesn't know it is part of a tree.' He meant that you don't know your 'roots': your ancestors. And to delve into history is to discover your roots, your culture.

If only I'd known this in my young days. How I was taught history in school failed to stir any spark of interest in me for the subject. Having to recall the many battles and their dates in order to pass the final school exams left me cold and uninterested. I left school never realizing that the 1916 Rising actually failed. I grew up believing the GPO garrison – which I'm proud to say included my own great-grandfather – had defeated the British forces.

Thankfully, I have since discovered my love of researching local and social history despite my earlier experience in school. I am lucky to be living in a county that played a pivotal role in shaping the Ireland of today. Wexford's history is indeed fascinating, with an abundance of tales of heroism, tragedy and momentous events. Spanning 1,200 years – from the 9th to the 20th centuries – this second volume of *Fascinating Wexford History* covers a wide spectrum, from violent murders and hangings to haunted houses, movie-making and the peace and tranquility of living on a 300-year-old farm.

I have written about some of Wexford's connections with both world wars: the heroism of a Duncormick native in WWI, immortalized as the 'Angel of Mons', and the torpedoing of German U-boats off Hook Head by the US Navy. Wexford's slave-labourers in a Nazi concentration camp during WWII and the virtually forgotten sinking of the Rosslare-Fishguard ferry by the Luftwaffe are included.

The assassination in Gorey of an RIC inspector by Michael Collins' hit squad during the War of Independence is an intriguing story that ended with his widow unwittingly purchasing a Caravaggio masterpiece, valued today at over €100 million.

This collection of illustrated stories includes an exorcism, witchcraft and a visit from the Devil, as well as tales from the Viking and later Anglo-Norman settlement of the county. Who knew that Selskar Abbey was the site of the first ever Anglo-Irish peace treaty?

I hope you enjoy what I believe is a fresh approach to recalling these events from Wexford's fascinating past in an attractive format. You are a leaf of the tree, whose roots lie in the pages of history.

Pirates, mutiny and hidden treasure on the Hook Peninsula

WE MAY ASSOCIATE pirates with the Caribbean and other warmer parts of the world but over the centuries the south coast of Ireland was a prime hunting area for pirates, privateers and smugglers. Raids on ships on the American trade route to Britain, Spain, France or Holland were commonplace. By the 1600s, Wexford had become a notorious haven of international piracy.

DOLLAR BAY

The *Earl of Sandwich* was spotted on 6 December 1765 near Broomhill Point on the west coast of the Hook Peninsula in an area now known as Dollar Bay. The mystery ship had no crew on board and the deck-boat was missing. It was half submerged and breaking up in what appeared to be a failed attempt at deliberately sinking the vessel.

Named after the 17th century naval officer and politician, Admiral Sir Edward Montagu, the *Earl of Sandwich* left the Canary Islands bound for England, under the command of Captain John Cochran. The ship had been summoned to pick up Scotsman George Glas, himself a sea captain, along with his wife and 11-year-old daughter Kathleen. Glas was a privateer who had made his fortune in the West Indies. He had also discovered a lucrative harbour, which he was developing in partnership with others in the Cape Verde Islands off the coast of northwest Africa. But on a trip in a open boat to the Canary Islands out of necessity to procure provisions from the Spaniards, he was arrested, accused of spying and thrown in jail and was kept there for several months. When the authorities in England received the news, an application was made to King Carlos III of Spain for his release.

The *Earl of Sandwich* set sail from London in July 1765 and on arrival at Tenerife, took on a cargo the equivalent of £100,000 in Spanish gold and silver dollars, a number of gold bars, some jewellery and a small quantity of gold dust. Spanish gold and silver dollars were widely used as an international currency and in order to make change during purchases, the dollars were often cut into eight pieces, giving the coins the alternative name 'pieces of eight'. Captain Glas and his wife also brought their servant boy on board for the journey back to London. The ship's officer or boatswain was Peter McKinlie, who hailed from Donegal, and the cook was George Gidley from Yorkshire. There were five other crew members including another Yorkshireman, Richard St. Quintin and 24-year-old Andres Zekerman from Holland. The ship's mates were Charles Pinchent and his brother James. Also on board was cabin boy Benjamin Gallipsey.

Before leaving Tenerife in November 1765, McKinlie, Gidley, St. Quintin and Zekerman hatched a plan to kill all on board and make off with the treasure, worth more than £20 million in today's terms, before reaching England. The valuable cargo was stored away for safe-keeping. Having set sail, Captain Cochran remained vigilant and observed the crew at all times throughout the voyage. On three separate nights the men attempted to carry out their plan but were thwarted on

Mrs. Glas and daughter Kathleen plead with the pirates to spare their lives on board the Earl of Sandwich.

each occasion by Cochran's watchful eye. Finally, around midnight on the night of 30 November, when they had reached the English Channel on course for London, Cochran was returning from the quarter-deck when McKinlie pulled him to the ground. Gidley struck him with an iron bar, fracturing his skull, and the two men threw him overboard.

Glas appeared from his quarters and, seeing there had been a mutiny, returned to fetch his sword. But McKinlie waited in the dark with a drawn sword until he returned, and grabbed him from behind. As Zekerman approached, he was wounded in the arm but Glas dropped his sword. Before he could recover it, Gidley and St. Quintin overpowered him and ran it several times through his body, after which he too was thrown overboard. The Pinchent brothers were likewise attacked and they too were overpowered and thrown into the sea. When Mrs. Glas and her daughter arrived on deck, they fell to their knees and pleaded for mercy. But Zekerman told them to prepare to die and as they were locked in one other's arms, were thrown overboard together.

With only the cabin boy Benjamin Gallipsey and the servant boy surviving, the mutineers turned the *Earl of Sandwich* around and steered towards the Wexford coast. On Tuesday 3 December at around 6pm they had passed Hook Head, heading towards New Ross. They decided to then launch the ship's longboat and loaded it with two tonnes of coins and treasure. Leaving the two boys on board, they then knocked out the ballast-port windows in order to scuttle the ship. The servant boy was unable to swim and drowned as the ship filled with water. The cabin boy Benjamin swam to the boat as the four prepared to row away but Zekerman struck him violently in the chest and he disappeared beneath the water.

Having now killed eight on board the ship, the four decided to land on the beach at what is now known as Dollar Bay, a couple of miles south of Duncannon. There they buried 250 bags of dollar coins in the sand and proceeded with the remaining coins, jewels and gold dust and landed the longboat at Fisherstown, about four miles before New Ross. They found the nearest inn and while enjoying a meal, a bag containing a thousand dollars was stolen from them. Next day they continued on to New Ross and at an alehouse exchanged 1,200 dollars and bought themselves a pair of pistols each. On 5 December, they hired six horses for themselves and two guides and set out for Dublin. Arriving the next day, Friday, they took lodgings at the Black Bull Inn on Thomas Street.

Meanwhile, the wreck of the *Earl of Sandwich*, which was presumed to have sunk, was driven ashore at Dollar Bay on the day after the men left New Ross. It was boarded and searched by customs officials, who suspected that the ship had been plundered by pirates. They searched the ship for clues and found a piece of embroidery worked by young Kathleen Glas. It appeared to have been made on her birthday, the day before the murders. Suspicion was immediately directed towards the four men who had recently been spending lavishly in the locality. Two agents were sent to inform the chief magistrate in New Ross.

In Dublin, St. Quintin and Zekerman were arrested and questioned separately. Each confessed to the murders and theft. A few guineas, a gold bar and a small parcel of gold dust were found in their possession. Questioned as to the whereabouts of the other two accomplices, they admitted that Gidley and McKinlie had sold a large amount of Spanish dollars to a goldsmith in the city. Gidley was apprehended and he admitted that McKinlie had left Dublin by hired carriage for Cork, from where he intended fleeing to England. All three confessed that they had buried much of their booty at Dollar Bay. The two agents relayed this information back to New Ross authorities who directed the commanding officer at Duncannon Fort to recover the buried treasure. On 13 December, the 250 bags of dollars were found and removed under guard to the custom house in New Ross.

Dollar Bay, where the abandoned 'Earl of Sandwich' was discovered breaking up, having run ashore on 6 December 1765. Pirates had buried two tonnes of Spanish dollars here in the sand. (photo: Des Kiely)

On their way back from Dublin, the two customs agents caught up with McKinlie on the road to Cork. He was committed to Carlow jail and on him were found 53 guineas, a Portuguese gold coin and some silver.

On Saturday 1 March 1766, the four prisoners were brought to trial, confessed their guilt and were all condemned to death. They were publicly hanged at St. Stephen's Green on Monday 3 March. Their bodies were then returned to Newgate prison, originally a gate in the city wall near Christ Church Cathedral that marked the western boundary. On Wednesday, the bodies of St. Quintin and Zekerman were hung in chains from a scaffold near Macarrell's Wharf (now Sir John Rogerson's Quay) as a warning to others. The bodies of McKinlie and Gidley were hung in chains close to the house of John Pidgeon at the South Wall. Pidgeon was caretaker of the South Wall and also ran a teahouse for sightseers. Today this is the site of the Pigeon House power station. According to *Faulkner's Journal*, following complaints by the public, the bodies of the four pirates were carried by sea to The Muglins rock near Dalkey Island on 1 April. There they we hung up in irons from a scaffold.

For years after, people searched the shoreline between New Ross and the Hook for any hidden treasure that may not have been retrieved. It was also believed that some of the gold went down with the ship and the area around Dollar Bay was trawled for years after in the hope of dragging up some Spanish silver dollars.

PIRATE LAFFAN OF SLADE

Slade Harbour, located one mile from Hook Lighthouse, is the only natural harbour on the peninsula. In 1290, Henry II granted the Hook lands to the military and religious order, the Knights Templar. The Laffans landed as part of the Anglo-Norman invasion and were tenants on the Knights' manor of Kilcloggan. In the late 1400s, the Laffans built Slade Castle, which had strategic views over the English Channel as well as Bannow Bay and the Suir estuary. However, their 210-acre holding was modest and there were questions as to how the impressive fortification was funded. It was believed that, apart from fishing, their main source of revenue must have been smuggling and piracy.

Known locally as 'Pirate Laffan', this noted smuggler would regularly climb

Slade Castle engraving by Francis Grose from his 'Antiquities of Ireland' published in 1791.

to the lookout platform of the castle, from where for hours he observed every ship that passed. One particular vessel appeared now and then, signalled by a red lantern that Laffan erected to indicate the castle's location. The ship would call into the harbour but be gone again by morning. This vessel, locals assumed, was engaged in smuggling. Nobody knew who Pirate Laffan really was and his true identity was not revealed for many years. His outer appearance was that of a handsome man, perhaps of nobility. Although in the prime of his life, he also seemed troubled by some tragedy in his past.

The mystery ship was present in Slade Bay one night when a stranger on horseback called to the castle. Claiming to have an important letter for Laffan, he was ushered inside. But when Laffan appeared, the unknown visitor immediately drew his pistol, shot him dead and rode off into the night. Witnesses said they noticed that half of the killer's right arm was missing. The ship left Slade the following morning carrying Laffan's body and was never seen in the area again.

The murder remained unsolved until years later when a document was found in the castle. This revealed Laffan's true identity. His real name was Vincente della Ronda, a 16th century privateer from Saragossa, the capital of the Kingdom of Aragon in northeast Spain. He came from a wealthy family but when his father died when he was just nine years old, leaving no lawful heir, the family property passed to someone outside the family. Vincente and his mother moved farther south to Daroca and when he was older he became engaged in privateering and smuggling. He was also involved in taking Irish refugees fleeing religious persecution to Spain.

Vincente, on a visit to Saragossa, called to his ancestral home once more and met its new owner, Don Álvaro. Having been invited into his old house, he was introduced to Álvaro's beautiful 18-year-old daughter, Ignessa. The two fell in love and Vincente pledged to return when he had made his fortune in privateering.

However, an Englishman by the name of Algernon Morcombe was also to enter Ignessa's life. He warned her that Vincente was a pirate who had attacked and plundered a ship he once sailed on from England to Spain. Only Morcombe and another sailor survived the ordeal. When Vincente called again to see his beloved Ignessa, he came upon Morcombe. A sword fight ensued in which Morcombe lost his right arm below the elbow. Morcombe swore he would exact revenge one day.

Vincente and Ignessa decided to elope. Having boarded a boat to reach the ship that they would leave on, her father Don Álvaro spotted the pair and swam after them. He pleaded with Ignessa not to leave and pulled her into the water. They both drowned. Broken-hearted, Vincente returned to sea and eventually ended up in Slade Castle, from where he continued his privateering and smuggling activities. Algernon Morcombe finally tracked him down on that fateful night when he carried out his promised revenge.

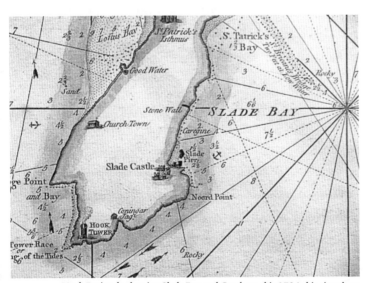

Hook Peninsula showing Slade Bay and Castle on this 1794 shipping chart.

The Catholic Laffan family were dispossessed of Slade Castle following the Confederate Rebellion of 1641 and the subsequent arrival of Cromwellian forces in Wexford in 1649. The castle and lands were granted to the Loftus family, who built the first harbour pier in 1684.

SALTEE ISLANDS

According to Philip Hore's 1901 book, *History of the Town and County of Wexford,* the channel between the Saltees and the mainland was once 'swarming with pirates'. The islands were used as a base for buccaneers, wreckers and smugglers all through the medieval era and right up to the 1700s. From the 15th

The Saltee Islands were a haven for pirates. Some actually lived there for part of the year. (photo: © Saltee Islands)

century, the islands found themselves in the path of a major trading route between Britain and its new American colonies and ships were plundered by pirates from Spain, France and Africa. The treacherous waters around the islands were known as 'the graveyard of a thousand ships' and locals helped themselves to salvage from the many shipwrecks.

The booty of the pirates and smugglers could be well hidden in the many caves on the Saltees. Some believe that treasure may still lie in locations on Great Saltee that bear mysterious names such as Hell Hole, Happy Hole, Otter's Cave and Lady Walker's Cave.

Privateers operated out of Wexford Harbour with impunity during the Confederate Wars that began in 1641, when Catholics tried to seize control of the English administration in Ireland. They sailed on armed ships owned and crewed by Irish, French and Flemish individuals and authorized by the Catholic Confederation. They attacked and captured English vessels at sea, from the Bay of Biscay to the Baltics, and were permitted to keep any stolen cargoes on their return. The Confederates had control of Wexford town, which became enriched by the privateers. Hore wrote: *'Besides the foreign pirates who preyed upon the merchant vessels of both countries, there were a score of fast-sailing frigates and sloops in Wexford Harbour, well manned and equipped, and their masters, who knew every rock and shoal around the south-east coast, were continually at war with the Parliament ships.'* In 1649, Cromwell's army landed in Dublin, soon marched on Wexford and decisively crushed the Confederates, putting an end to its privateering.

Seán Etchingham, Enniscorthy: 'one day of blissful freedom'

Leaders of the Volunteers being led away from the Athenaeum in Enniscorthy by army officers on 1 May 1916, having just surrendered. The picture was taken by local photographer Alfred E. Crane from Court Street.

ON DAY ONE of the Rising in Enniscorthy, 27 April 1916, Volunteer Seán Etchingham wrote in his diary: "We had at least one day of blissful freedom. We have had Enniscorthy under the laws of the Irish Republic for at least one day and it pleases me to learn that the citizens are appreciably surprised. The people of the town are great. The manhood of Enniscorthy is worthy of its manhood."

Outside Dublin, Enniscorthy was the only town or city to be seized by the Volunteers in the course of the Easter Rising. Some 1,000 insurgents held the town for four days. A member of the RIC and two civilians were wounded by gunfire but there were no fatalities. "We closed the public houses. We established a force of Irish Republican police, comprising some of Enniscorthy's most respectable citizens, and a more orderly town could not be imagined," wrote Etchingham.

Born John Redmond Hutchingham in Ballinatray townland, Courtown, in 1870 to John and Elizabeth (née Redmond), he left school at the age of 14 and first worked as a clerk at the Courtown Brick and Tile Works. In the census of 1901, Seán gives his name as Etchingham and his profession as horse trainer with an address at Church Lane, Gorey but 10 years later he was back living in Courtown and declared his profession to be that of a journalist.

The Gaelic League was founded in 1893 with the aim of restoring the Irish language and culture. It did not gain a foothold in County Wexford until about 1900 and Seán became an enthusiastic member and even founded a local branch. He started writing for the *Enniscorthy Echo,* a paper that supported radical republicanism, under the name Patsy Patrick. He wrote on sport, culture and politics as well as penning witty articles about everyday life.

Seán was also an enthusiastic member of the GAA in north Wexford and in 1902-4 – and again in 1919-22 – was chairman of the Wexford County Board. Etchingham and others were attempting to push the association towards a more radical nationalist position. Members of the GAA who played or watched 'foreign games' such as cricket, rugby, soccer or tennis were barred under the 'ban' rules. Enniscorthy Volunteers GAA club members who attended a rugby match in 1913 were suspended. When another member, Robert Hanlon, was expelled for attending a rugby club dance, he sought re-admission through a friend who said Hanlon did not believe he had done anything wrong. "He must come here and express his regret and make an apology", said Etchingham. "What is the Association coming to? Here we have a man breaking the rules, and afterwards seeking to be re-admitted!", said his friend and fellow GAA official Pádraig Kehoe. Another Enniscorthy player, Aidan Connolly, having won seven senior football championships, played for Enniscorthy Rugby Club in 1913 in a game against Lansdowne and was suspended for a year.

While Wexford politics in the early part of the 1900s was dominated by the Irish Parliamentary Party, Enniscorthy had a strong Irish Republican Brotherhood presence, led by Larry de Lacey. The Irish Volunteers, the military organization made up of members of the Irish Republican Brotherhood, the Gaelic League, the Ancient Order of Hibernians and Sinn Féin, were established in 1913. Enniscorthy had about 100 members but there was a split the following year when the First World War broke out. Wexford's John Redmond, leader of the Irish Parliamentary Party, was urging members of the Volunteers to join the British Army in the hope of gaining Home

Seán Etchingham, a native of Courtown, was one of the leaders of the Enniscorthy Rising.

Rule for Ireland. The Home Rule Act 1914 was already on the statute books. A minority opted for offensive action at home while Britain was tied up in the war in Europe. Charlie Farrell, a local veteran of the Fenian Rising of 1867, is quoted as saying: "Ireland will never be free until Enniscorthy and every other Irish town runs red with blood."

In November 1914, Seán Etchingham suggested that Wexford GAA should establish rifle clubs and this was met with general agreement. With a shortage of arms, Enniscorthy battalion members were threatened with disciplinary action if they were caught attending dances instead of contributing the money to the arms fund.

Thomas MacDonagh, who would later be executed as one of the leaders of the 1916 Rising in Dublin, sent IRB man Paul Galligan to Enniscorthy "to take charge of advanced training". Enniscorthy was seen as a strategic military location, being on the railway route from Rosslare to Dublin, which would carry British soldiers following the outbreak of the planned rising in the capital. Galligan used the alias *O'Reilly* and took a job in Bolger's drapery shop. He trained Volunteers in a house on Mary Street they nicknamed *Antwerp*, where munitions were also made.

In March 1916, Pádraig Pearse visited Enniscorthy for a commemoration of Robert Emmet, who was hanged in Dublin following his failed rebellion in 1803. He gave a lecture at a concert held in the Athenaeum theatre on Castle Street. The Enniscorthy battalion supplied him a guard of honour and had the building under armed guard in case of any interference by the RIC. In private, Pearse told Volunteer officers to expect orders soon for an armed uprising.

ENNISCORTHY RISING

Antrim native Eoin MacNeill, chief-of-staff of the Irish Volunteers, saw little hope of success in an armed rebellion against the mighty British Army. But Pearse saw Britain's participation in WWI as a perfect opportunity to launch an uprising in Ireland. On behalf of the IRB, he ordered Volunteers throughout the country to take part in three days of 'parades and manoeuvres' beginning on Easter Sunday, 23 April 1916. This was Pearse's coded signal for armed rebellion. Assured that Roger Casement was due to arrive in County Kerry on board a German submarine to rendezvous with a shipment of arms from Germany on Good Friday, O'Neill reluctantly went along with the plan.

But the German ship, the *Aud,* failed to meet with Casement, who was arrested. The *Aud* was trapped in a blockade of British ships. While being towed into Queenstown (Cobh) Harbour, it was scuttled using pre-set explosive charges. Casement was later hanged for treason in England in August 1916.

Eoin O'Neill, on hearing of the loss of the arms and ammunition on Saturday, placed an advertisement in the *Sunday Independent* the next day with the headline: "No Parades! Irish Volunteer Marches Cancelled". As a result, many Volunteers changed their plans for Easter weekend, some heading off on their Easter break. But Pearse would not relent.

This resulted in great confusion among the Volunteers throughout the country, with contradictory orders coming from Dublin. J.J. 'Ginger' O'Connell, a member of the Volunteers who had spent some time in the U.S. Army, had been put in command of the rising in the south-east. He now told the Enniscorthy officers Seamus Rafter, Seamus Doyle and Paul Galligan that "he would take no part in the forthcoming rising and, further, it would be our responsibility whatever action we took."

Paul Galligan travelled to Dublin late on Easter Saturday night to find out what was happening. He was told that the Rising was cancelled and stayed overnight in a house in Dalkey. The next morning, on hearing of events in Sackville Street, he met with James Connolly, Patrick Pearse and Joseph Plunkett in the GPO. Only about a quarter of the 10,000 Volunteers who might have been deployed were now participating in the Rising.

Connolly instructed Galligan to return to Enniscorthy to cut the railway line and prevent British reinforcements getting through to Dublin via the ports of Rosslare and Waterford. He was given a 'good bicycle' from the GPO storehouse and headed off at first light on Tuesday 25 April. To avoid British troops, he embarked on a 120-mile cycle trip through counties Kildare and Carlow, arriving in Enniscorthy late on Wednesday evening.

In the meantime, Seamus Doyle had received instructions from Pearse on

Easter Monday afternoon telling the Enniscorthy Volunteers: "we start at noon today, obey your orders". Doyle was unclear what the orders were and asked Seán Sinnott, who was commander of the brigade in Wexford town. Sinnott declared "in consequence of the conflicting orders I will not have anything to do with the matter". When Galligan returned to Enniscorthy a meeting was called in *Antwerp* on Wednesday night, where he relayed instructions from Dublin and news of the Rising already underway. The decision was made to launch the rebellion.

At daybreak the next morning Thursday 27 April (the fourth day of the Rising in Dublin), the Enniscorthy Volunteers gathered at 10 Irish Street, the house of Pat Keegan, quartermaster for the brigade. There they collected 20 rifles and 2,000 rounds of ammunition. About 90 Volunteers, some symbolically carrying pikes, marched to the Athenaeum which they made their command centre. The terraced street location was preferred over Enniscorthy Castle, which was considered to be too exposed and vulnerable to attack by British artillery.

Around 8am, the Volunteers stopped people as they headed to work and told them that there would be no work that day as the Republic was proclaimed, so they all returned home. Seán Etchingham took over the banks, telling the managers to lock up everything. The RIC were confined to barracks. Notices were pasted around the town, instructing anyone with firearms to hand them in before noon. Public houses were ordered to close. Checkpoints were set up on all approach roads into the town and permission had to be sought from headquarters in the Athenaeum by anybody wishing to leave. Telegraph and telephone wires were cut and business in the town suspended. Food supplies, bedding and clothing were seized from shops with receipts issued and the Volunteers took possession of a number of motor vehicles.

The Athenaeum theatre on Castle Street was the chosen location of the Enniscorthy Volunteers for the duration of the four-day rising in 1916.

They also occupied the railway station. They commandeered a train that was on its way from Wexford to Arklow with 300 workmen, heading for Kynoch's munitions factory. With WWI underway in Europe, Kynoch's employed 5,000 people working around the clock. Special trains were in service to transport workers from as far south as Wexford town. The Volunteers permitted those on board to walk back to Wexford alongside the railway line and they detached the steam engine from the train. Signalling wires were cut and railway lines at either end of the town torn up.

Seán Etchingham was in charge of recruiting. Men from Ferns and Gorey as well as local men and boys wanted to join the rebels. The old RIC barracks became a recruiting office. Some 1,000 took part and most were in uniform, and town patrols were established. A 10pm curfew was ordered and a warning issued that anyone caught looting would be shot on sight.

Among the commanders in the Athenaeum were Seamus Rafter, Paul Galligan, Robert Brennan, Seamus Doyle, Richard King, Michael de Lacy and Seán Etchingham. A local priest, Father Patrick Murphy, publicly blessed the rebels. About 70 or 80 women, including 30 members of Cumann na mBan, the female auxiliary of the Irish Volunteers, set up an emergency hospital and kitchen in the building. Among them were Una Brennan, Greta Comerford and Marion Stokes. Paul Galligan ordered a guard of honour as the three women raised the tricolour on the roof. Seamus Doyle read the Proclamation of the Republic. A number of rebels had also taken up positions around the ruined windmill on Vinegar Hill. (Una Brennan was married to Robert Brennan and Greta Comerford married Seamus Doyle in 1918).

THE SURRENDER

Pádraig Pearse surrendered in Dublin on Saturday 29 April after five days and nights of fighting "to prevent the further slaughter of the civilian population and in the hope of saving our followers, now hopelessly surrounded and outnumbered." On the same day, the fourth day of the Enniscorthy rising, news reached the Volunteers that the British garrison in Arklow was preparing to move south to carry out an assault. Galligan and about 50 men travelled to Ferns to set up an outpost. They occupied the national school and RIC barracks, already vacated by the police.

The British War Office contacted Roscommon-born Colonel George

A group of Volunteers and Cumann na mBan members pose in the Athenaeum just before their surrender on 1 May 1916. Front row (l-r): Seamus Rafter (Enniscorthy), Robert Brennan (Wexford), Seamus Doyle (Ferns), Seán Etchingham (Gorey). Back row: Una Brennan (Oylegate), Michael de Lacey (Oulart) and Eileen O'Hegarty.

French, a retired British Army Officer who lived in Newbay House outside Wexford town. He was requested to take command of the British Forces in Wexford. Reinforcements were already on their way by military armoured train from Waterford, carrying a fifteen-pounder field gun they nicknamed *'Enniscorthy Emily'*. In Wexford town French assembled a force of about 1,000 men, including a mobile column that had landed from Queenstown, a naval gun and a second field gun, and headed towards Enniscorthy, stopping about six miles south of the town. He sent word ahead that the insurgents should surrender and avoid loss of life and damage to property if he had to shell the town. He had good local knowledge and knew how to handle the situation.

By Sunday morning there was no sign of either the Arklow garrison or the force from Wexford moving on Enniscorthy. Later that afternoon, an RIC District Inspector and Sergeant arrived from Dublin under armed escort and handed in a copy of Pearse's surrender. But the Volunteers were sceptical. Seamus Doyle and Seán Etchingham requested permission from Colonel French to travel to Dublin and meet Pearse in person. He agreed and supplied a military car that drove them to Arbour Hill prison, where Pearse was being held. Pearse was not aware of the rising in Enniscorthy but he confirmed the surrender in writing for Doyle and Etchingham to take back to Enniscorthy.

A blank shell from the British field gun 'Enniscorthy Emily' was fired in the direction of the 200 or so insurgents who were positioned on Vinegar Hill. They hoisted a white flag and dispersed but many were captured. The others laid down their arms unconditionally.

When Doyle and Etchingham arrived back in Enniscorthy the next day, Monday 1 May, the Volunteers formally surrendered to Colonel French. The leaders were treated with respect by French, who was described as a gentleman and whose family was well respected in the county. They were marched away and taken to Dublin. In all, 375 insurgents were arrested and 319 sent to Dublin. The police seized 46 rifles, 66 shotguns, 8 pistols, 6 revolvers, 1 bomb, 21 stone of blasting powder, 667 rounds of sporting ammunition, 4,067 rounds of rifle and revolver ammunition, as well as gelignite and other explosives.

Not all of the town had supported the rebellion and soon RIC and British troops were patrolling the town, helped by local 'Redmondites'. Outside of Enniscorthy the population was generally hostile to the rebels and some 'Home Rulers' took up arms to assist the British to round up Republicans.

Seán Etchingham was sentenced to death by a court-martial. His response was to sarcastically enquire if he could be let off under the First Offenders Act. His sentence was eventually commuted to five years and he was sent to Dartmoor Prison. But while he lingered in prison, Seán must have been thrilled on hearing one piece of good news from home a week before Christmas 1916. His beloved Wexford team had beaten Mayo by 3-4 to 1-2 and retained the All-Ireland senior football championship. Before being released under the General Amnesty of all Irish Republican prisoners in 1917 however, Seán contracted tuberculosis while in jail.

In the December 1918 general election Sinn Féin beat the Irish Parliamentary Party in a landslide victory. Etchingham won a seat for Sinn Féin representing Wicklow East. Independence from Britain was declared in January 1919, ratifying the proclamation of an Irish Republic that had been issued in the Easter Rising. A provisional government was formed and on the day that the first Dáil sat, the War of Independence broke out with the killing of two RIC officers by Volunteers in the Soloheadbeg ambush in County Tipperary. The Dáil was outlawed by the British government in September 1919, and thereafter met in secret. Etchingham was appointed Minister for

Fisheries in November 1919. In the same month he became the first Sinn Féin chairman of Wexford County Council.

During the War of Independence, which lasted until July 1921, the notorious reserve force, the Black and Tans, were recruited into the RIC. Martial law was declared in County Wexford in January 1921 and in May, the Black and Tans attacked and destroyed Etchingham's house in Courtown. In the same month, he was returned as one of four Sinn Féin members for Wexford in the uncontested general election.

Etchingham opposed the signing of the Anglo-Irish Treaty of 1921 that sparked the 1922-3 Civil War. During fighting, two Volunteers were killed in a shoot-out between anti-Treaty and Free State troops at Enniscorthy Castle. Seán Etchingham lay in a Dublin nursing home for several months, suffering from tuberculosis. As the war continued into 1923, he was brought home to Courtown to die. From there he sent a message to the Wexford GAA County Board, saying he was heartbroken "at the continuance of the present differences among Irishmen who had done so much in the past for the uplifting of our motherland". He died on 23 April 1923, exactly one week before a nationwide ceasefire was called by the anti-Treaty side.

The Athenaeum was extensively restored and refurbished in 2016 and houses County Wexford's 1916 archive collection of artefacts and documents.

Members of the First Dáil outside the Mansion House, Dublin. Seán Etchingham is in the back row, second from left.

Garda hurling champion shot dead by IRA near Cleariestown

The scene of the shoot-out at Ballyconnick quarry on the day after Garda Seamus Quaid was murdered.

SINCE THE establishment of An Garda Síochána in 1922 a total of 88 members have died while on duty. At least 30 were murdered and 23 of these were killed by republican paramilitary individuals or a group. Detective Garda Seamus Quaid was shot dead by a member of the Provisional IRA during an exchange of gunfire, after stopping a vehicle containing explosives near Cleariestown, County Wexford in 1980.

Born in County Limerick in 1937, Seamus Quaid joined the Gardaí and in 1958, aged 20, was posted to Wexford. He married local woman Olive O'Neill, who worked at Pierce's Foundry. They had four children and lived on St. Brendan's Road in the Maudlinstown area of Wexford town. Seamus came from a family with a proud hurling tradition and he joined the Faythe Harriers shortly after arriving in the town. He was part of the County Wexford team that won the 1960 All-Ireland Senior Hurling Championship after defeating Tipperary by 2-15 to 0-11, with Seamus playing at wing forward and scoring 2 points in the game.

In 1979, Seamus was appointed to the Detective Branch based in Wexford Garda Station on Roche's Road. This was at the height of the Troubles in

Northern Ireland, which at times spilled over into regions of the Republic. As part of his duties, Detective Garda Seamus Quaid and his unit were keeping an eye on local republican activities in the Wexford area. Armed bank robberies were regularly carried out by paramilitary groups to fund their campaigns in Northern Ireland and England. In July 1980, two Gardaí, Henry Byrne and John Morley, both County Mayo natives, were murdered in a shootout with members of the INLA following a bank robbery in Ballaghaderreen, County Roscommon. Detective Morley, who had been armed with an Uzi submachine gun, was regarded as one of Mayo GAA's greatest footballers. His championship career with the Mayo senior team spanned thirteen seasons between 1961 and 1974.

On 17 January 1972, seven republican internees escaped from the reputedly escape-proof British prison ship, HMS *Maidstone*, which was moored in Belfast docks. They swam 400 yards in bitterly cold water, their bodies smeared with butter and boot polish to insulate them. Once on land they commandeered a bus and one of the escapees, Peter Rogers, a former bus driver, took the wheel and they made their escape through the city. Within a few days, all seven appeared at a press conference in Dublin, from where they, as political prisoners, could not be extradited.

Wexford All-Ireland Senior Hurling Champions 1960.
Back row: Padge Kehoe, Tom Neville, J. Nolan, Nick O'Donnell (Captain), Tim Flood, Billy Rackard,
Ned Wheeler, Jim Morrissey. Front: Jim English, John Mitchell, Pat Nolan, Jimmy O'Brien, Jack Harding,
Oliver Hopper McGrath, Seamus Quaid.

Rogers settled and married in County Wexford but remained an active member of the IRA. He lived in a mobile home in Knocktown, between Cleariestown and Duncormick, with his wife and young child and drove a vegetable delivery van for a living. He was a familiar face in the Wexford area.

Detective Garda Seamus Quaid, aged 42, was gunned down while on duty by IRA activist Peter Rogers near Cleariestown in 1980.

On 13 October 1980, an armed gang got away with £9,000 when they raided two banks in Callan, County Kilkenny. The Gardaí in Wexford were asked to check on a car believed to have been used in the robbery. Garda Donal Lyttleton and Garda Seamus Quaid, both armed, wanted to interview known republican activists in the Wexford area, including 36-year-old Peter Rogers, who had now been living in the Wexford area for six years and whom they both knew.

They called twice to his mobile home on the same day as the Kilkenny robberies but got no reply and decided to return to Wexford Garda Station. At about 10.30pm they passed Peter Roger's Transit van travelling in the opposite direction on a dark isolated road. They turned their car and followed, signalling him to stop. He finally pulled in at Ballinconnick quarry near Cleariestown.

All three men got out of their vehicles, with Lyttleton leaving his gun behind in the car. The Gardaí told Rogers they wanted to search his van. When they opened it they found a large consignment of guns and explosives hidden behind sacks of potatoes in the back. Rogers suddenly pulled a gun and told them to move back towards the quarry. Garda Quaid drew his gun and after a total of ten shots were fired in a shoot-out with Rogers, he lay mortally wounded on the ground. Lyttleton managed to escape on foot to raise the alarm. Despite having been shot in the foot and with a punctured tyre from the crossfire, Rogers fled in his van. One of the bullets that penetrated Seamus Quaid's leg had severed his femorel artery; assistance did not get to him on time and he bled to death within about 15 minutes.

Rogers, wounded and panicking, pulled up at a neighbour's farmhouse, wielding a gun and demanding a car. He warned the family not to report the incident until the following day and drove into Wexford town. Bizarrely, he called to the home of Seamus Quaid's friend and hurling team-mate Ned Wheeler, who lived on Fisher's Row, not far from Seamus's own house. Wheeler won three All-Ireland medals with Wexford in 1955, 1956 and on the same team as Seamus in 1960. He was a customer of Rogers, who claimed his foot got caught in the accelerator pedal in a traffic accident, and so Ned gave him a bed in his house for the night.

The following morning Wexford woke up to the shocking news of the murder. Seamus Quaid was very popular, not only as a county and All-Ireland hurler, but as a Garda too. When Ned Wheeler realized that he'd harboured his friend's killer he asked Rogers to give himself up. Accompanied by a priest, Rogers entered Wexford Garda Station and surrendered. Later that day he was formally charged with the murder at a special sitting of the District Court. Rogers was taken to Wexford County Hospital to be treated for his gunshot wound while Seamus Quaid was laid out in the hospital mortuary.

People lined the streets of Wexford on the day of Seamus Quaid's funeral, one of the biggest the town had seen. Huge crowds came out to witness the procession as it made its way from Bride Street church, over Wexford Bridge to Crosstown Cemetery. The Taoiseach, Charles Haughey, Fine Gael leader Garret Fitzgerald and senior members of the government were in attendance.

A Garda band leads the funeral cortège of Seamus Quaid past Wexford Garda Station on Roche's Road.

There was controversy when it emerged that Rogers had been mistakenly charged with common-law murder instead of capital murder. The case was brought up in the Dáil and the Taoiseach announced that the charge had since been struck out. Rogers was discharged from hospital on the same day as Seamus Quaid's funeral, three days after being admitted, and was immediately re-arrested and this time charged with capital murder.

In just three months, three Gardaí had been shot dead by republicans. Rogers' trial began in the Special Criminal Court in Dublin in February 1981 and lasted two weeks. He was found guilty of capital murder and sentenced to hang (capital punishment was not abolished in the Republic until 1990). This sentence was commuted by President Patrick Hillery to 40 years' imprisonment without remission.

The Gardaí believed that the guns and explosives were destined to be transported via Rosslare Port to England for a pre-Christmas bombing campaign. Therefore, by stopping Peter Rogers that October night in Cleariestown, many lives may well have been saved. A gold Scott Medal for bravery was posthumously awarded to Seamus Quaid in 1982 and accepted by his widow Olive. After serving nearly 18 years of his 40-year sentence, Peter Rogers was released from Portlaoise Prison in 1998 under the terms of the Good Friday Agreement. The Quaid family were upset at hearing of his release and Seamus Quaid's son Eamon told the *Sunday Independent:* "I know he has a son too in Wexford but he has been able to visit his father in prison. When I want to visit my dad, I can only go to his graveside."

Nine years into his sentence, Rogers left the republican movement, after writing to the Quaid family and Garda Lyttleton, apologizing for what he'd done but his apologies were not accepted. In 2014, Sinn Féin announced they were holding their *ard fheis* in the Wexford Opera House, where a nameplate to Garda Quaid was placed in 2008. Quaid's family complained that it was an insensitive choice of location and asked for the small plaque to be temporarily removed for the duration of the conference. Sinn Féin's Martin McGuinness said he was prepared to meet the Quaids and apologize for the killing but the family refused to meet him.

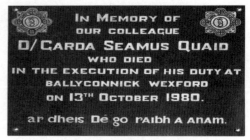

Memorial plaque in Wexford Garda Station.

The six Wexford people who sailed on Titanic

Passengers waiting at White Star Wharf, Queenstown (Cobh), Co. Cork, to embark on tenders taking them out to board Titanic, 11 April 1912. (photo: Fr. Francis Browne)

THE 'UNSINKABLE' *Titanic* sank on its maiden voyage from Southampton to New York having hit an iceberg in the North Atlantic at 11.40pm on 14 April 1912. The doomed liner left Southampton four days earlier, picking up passengers in Cherbourg and Queenstown (Cobh). Two tenders ferried 123 passengers, a mountain of luggage and 1,385 mailbags from the quay at Queenstown to *Titanic*, which was anchored off Roche's Point at the mouth of Cork Harbour. It set sail at 1.30pm on 11 April, heading for New York and carrying over 2,200 passengers and crew. Only 705 people would survive the impending tragedy. It took 73 years to find the wreckage, it being finally located by American oceanographer Dr. Robert Ballard in 1985.

Cork native Father Francis Browne, who lost both his parents as a child, was raised and supported by his uncle Robert Browne, Bishop of Cloyne. His uncle bought him his first camera and he went on to become a prolific photographer. In 1912, Francis received a present from his uncle: a ticket for the maiden voyage of *Titanic* from Southampton to Cobh. He took dozens of photographs on board *Titanic* and befriended a millionaire American couple who offered to pay his return fare to New York. Francis telegraphed his superior requesting permission to go, but received the terse reply: 'Get off that ship - Provincial.' Having disembarked at Cobh, Father Browne took one of the last known photographs of *Titanic* as it steamed out of Cork Harbour. In the same year that the wreck of the ship was found, a metal trunk containing Father Browne's fragile *Titanic* negatives was discovered in 1985. They were restored and published in 1997 as *Father Browne's Titanic Album*.

HUGH McELROY
Chief Purser *(Ballymitty, perished, aged 37)*

An old friend of Father Francis Browne was the ship's convivial and larger-than-life chief purser, Hugh McElroy, who had given the reverend permission to take photographs on board. Born in Liverpool into a Catholic family originally from Wexford, he went to sea at the age of 19 as assistant purser with the Allan Steamship Company on the advice of another friend: the shipping company's passenger manager, John Ennis. Six years later Hugh joined the White Star Line in 1899 and served on *Titanic*'s sister ship *Olympic*. Its captain was Edward Smith, who transferred along with McElroy as chief purser, to the newly-built *Titanic* for its maiden voyage in 1912.

When John Ennis retired, he returned to the extensive family farm, Springwood, on the Newline Road at Tullycanna near Ballymitty, County Wexford with his two daughters. Hugh married John's daughter Barbara, his childhood sweetheart, in St. Peter's Church in Ballymitty in 1910 and the ceremony was performed by Hugh's brother, Fr. Richard McElroy. The couple lived for a time at Springwood before moving to Southampton.

As chief purser, Hugh McElroy held a very important position on

Hugh McElroy with Captain Edward Smith before leaving Cobh on Titanic. Both were lost when it sank four days later. (photo: Cork Examiner)

This poignant image shows a funeral service, conducted by the ship's priest Reverend Hind on the deck of the Mackay Bennett, for dozens of victims of Titanic. Of the 1,517 who perished, they recovered 306 bodies and buried 116 at sea. The photograph only came to light in 2014 and was seen by the public for the first time.

board *Titanic*; he was the main link between passengers and crew and was a favourite of Captain Smith. With his charm and wit he was perfect for the job, with passengers passing him wireless messages for the Marconi room or handing in their valuables for safekeeping.

When the ship's engines stopped, having impacted with the iceberg, McElroy gave orders to crew members and got passengers to prepare to abandon ship, urging them to move to the upper deck. He assumed a position of power and was apparently passed a loaded revolver. Panic ensued as the last two lifeboats were being filled, and when two dining-room stewards jumped into one of the boats from the deck above, McElroy fired into the air and the pair were quickly thrown out of the boat.

As the last lifeboat pulled away, the ever-jovial McElroy is reported to have turned to his assistants and quipped: 'Well boys, the last boat has gone. I'm afraid we must eat sand for supper tonight.' Just minutes before the ship sank, he stood on the deck and shook hands with several colleagues including fellow Irishmen, Dr. William O'Loughlin from Tralee, the ship's senior surgeon, Dr. John Simpson from Belfast, assistant surgeon and Ernest King from

Galway, assistant purser. His body was recovered a week later and buried at sea along with 14 other victims. Approximately 334 bodies were recovered from the ocean — less than a quarter of the over 1,500 who died.

LIZZIE DOYLE
(Bree, perished, aged 26)

ROBERT MERNAGH
(Ballywilliam, perished, aged 28)

Lizzie emigrated to Philadelphia in 1909 but returned home to Bree two years later to nurse her widowed father Martin who was dying. She was the youngest daughter in the family, had a sunny disposition and was very popular in the district. After almost a year back home, her father died and Lizzie told friends that she intended to buy a second-class ticket for £10.10s on *Titanic* for her return trip. When news of the sinking reached Bree, there was great optimism that Lizzie was among the survivors because the crew of *Titanic* had allowed first-class women and children into the lifeboats first, then continued down the classes.

Lizzie's first cousin Robert Mernagh, from Ballywilliam near New Ross, had emigrated two years previously to Chicago, where his brother Matthew also lived. He too was home to visit family and may have delayed his return voyage in order to accompany his cousin back to America. They purchased third-class or steerage tickets costing £7.15s each from a New Ross agent.

They were both lost in the tragedy and if their bodies were recovered, were never identified. Lizzie's estate, valued at only £10, was granted to her brother Jeremiah, a postman, in 1913. Robert's estate, worth £30, went to his father Matthew. Lizzie is remembered in an inscription on her family's tombstone in St. David's Church Cemetery in Davidstown.

LARRY DOYLE
Stoker *(County Wexford, perished, aged 27)*

Larry was formerly employed as a stoker on the White Star Line's *Majestic*, which was at one time also commanded by Captain Edward Smith. He served too aboard *Lusitania*. On *Titanic* he was employed as a stoker for £6 a month. *Majestic* was taken out of service in 1911 but after *Titanic* sank, *Majestic* was put back into service as her replacement. Larry's birthplace is not known and his address was given locally as 10 Orchard Place, Southampton.

GEORGE McGOUGH
Able Seaman (*Duncannon, survived, aged 36*)

While serving on the *Rustington* in 1900, McGough killed another crew member, Welshman John Dwyer, in a drink-fuelled brawl on board while it was anchored off Santos near São Paulo, Brazil. He was convicted of manslaughter and served fifteen months' hard labour in Winchester Prison.

He signed up in Southampton for the ill-fated *Titanic* and was known on board

George McGough from Duncannon.

simply as 'Paddy'. After the ship collided with the iceberg, he managed to board one of the lifeboats with about 80 other survivors. Another crewman on the boat, George Kemish, later wrote: 'Paddy McGough suddenly gave a great shout: "Let us all pray to God, for there is a ship on the horizon and 'tis making for us." They were picked up by the *Carpathia* at about 7am. In an interview with the *Irish Independent* two weeks after the loss of *Titanic*, McGough stated: 'I saw Captain Smith, at some distance, swimming towards another boat. When they reached out to help him, he shouted at them: "Look out for yourselves men. Don't mind me. God bless you." Then he threw up his hand and disappeared.'

JOHN O'CONNOR
Coal Trimmer (*Coolcots, Wexford, survived, aged 25*)

The coal trimmer's job started with the loading of coal into the ship and ended with its delivery to the stoker or fireman, using shovels and wheelbarrows. *Titanic* had 73 trimmers aboard the coal-fed liner and only 20, including John O'Connor, survived. The trimmers were paid the least but O'Connor signed up in Southampton

Survivor John O'Connor from Coolcots, Wexford town.

for the maiden voyage of the largest ship afloat at the time, giving his local address as 9 Tower Place, Southampton. He previously worked on the *Olympic* and as a trimmer received a monthly wage of £5.10s. John probably thought himself lucky to have got on board as a substitute. Three brothers with the surname Slade missed boarding *Titanic* when a passing passenger train on the dock delayed them, causing them to miss reaching the gangway before it was raised. O'Connor and two others had taken their places.

Fellow crewman Jack Podesta told a newspaper reporter in 1968 that he remembered the Wexford town man and another trimmer, Wally Hurst, being picked up from a raft '...shivering terribly with cold. My mate and I gave them blankets and rubbed their legs to start up their circulation.' They too were eventually picked up by the *Carpathia* and, after a full recovery, John returned to England on the *Lapland*. He was the son of William O'Connor and Ann Cushen.

In all, 120 Irish people died on *Titanic* and 42 were saved. All 3 who were in first class died and only one of the 4 in second class survived. Of the 918 total staff and crew, 703 went down with the ship.

Father Browne's last photograph of Titanic as it sailed away from Cork Harbour on its final voyage.

Assassination in Gorey and a Caravaggio masterpiece

Capt. Percival Lea-Wilson and his executioner Liam Tobin.

IT IS ONE of the most extraordinary stories from the War of Independence (1919-21), one hundred years ago: the assassination in 1920 of 33-year-old Percival Lea-Wilson in Gorey by a hit squad sent by Michael Collins. Lea-Wilson was remembered for his ill-treatment of rebels, who had fought in the Four Courts and the GPO, following their surrender in 1916. His widow, Dr. Marie Lea-Wilson, purchased a painting at auction in 1924 and in 1990, it was identified as Caravaggio's masterpiece, *The Taking of Christ*.

Percival Lea-Wilson was born into a middle-class Protestant household in Kensington, London in 1887. The son of a stockbroker, he was the grandson of the Lord Mayor of London, Samuel Wilson. Although educated at Oxford, Percival chose a career in the Royal Irish Constabulary. He was first stationed in Woodford, Co. Galway and later in Charleville, Co. Cork in 1909, and in 1914 married a local Catholic girl Marie Ryan, the daughter of a well-known solicitor. At the outbreak of the First World War, he enlisted in the 18th Royal Irish Regiment and served on the Western Front, where he was seriously wounded. He had reached the rank of captain but his injury forced his return to Ireland.

According to RIC records, Lea-Wilson rejoined the police and was in Dublin during the 1916 Easter Rising. After six days of fighting, the Irish Volunteer garrison at the GPO surrendered to Brigadier-General Lowe, commander of British forces in Dublin.

My own great-grandfather, Luke Kennedy, was among those in the GPO who surrendered. He was a member of the Irish Republican Brotherhood from 1898 to 1922 and succeeded Major Seán McBride as leader of up to 100 mem-

Luke Kennedy was active in the GPO during the 1916 Rising and was among the Volunteers who surrendered and were held in the Rotunda Gardens under Captain Percival Lea-Wilson.

bers, who met under the guise of the 'Literary & Debating Society' at his house on Great Charles Street. On the fifth night of fighting, as Sackville Street and the upper floors of the GPO were engulfed in flames, the Volunteers made their way out onto Henry Street and into Moore Lane, evading British machine guns positioned at the end of the laneway and the top of Moore Street. Luke, along with Tom Clarke and other Volunteers, succeeded in breaking into a corner house on Moore Street and continued breaking through houses along the terrace until they reached a chemist shop, where they secured dressings for the wounded men. Number 16 Moore Street became their temporary headquarters for the night and it was there that the decision to surrender was made by Pádraig Pearse, James Connolly and Tom Clarke. The following afternoon, Pearse surrendered unconditionally to Brigadier-General Lowe at Clarke's little tobacconist shop on Great Britain Street (now Parnell Street).

Later that evening, the Volunteers marched up Moore Street and into Henry Street carrying their arms and equipment, turned left into Sackville Street and then across to the far side of the thoroughfare, where they were ordered to line up in single file. The British then instructed them to take three steps forward and lay down their arms. They were then marched to the Rotunda Gardens at the rear of the Rotunda Hospital, where they were kept for the remainder of the night. (Today this is the Garden of Remembrance, which was opened by President Éamon de Valera in 1966 and is dedicated to the memory of 'all those who gave their lives in the cause of Irish Freedom').

About 250 Volunteers were crammed into the garden where Captain Lea-

Wilson and his men walked amongst them. Lea-Wilson ordered that all the prisoners lie on the ground without moving for 12 hours, forcing them to relieve themselves where they lay. It is claimed that he picked out Tom Clarke, the first signatory on the Proclamation of the Republic, and marched him to the steps of the hospital and ordered soldiers to strip him naked as hospital staff looked on from the windows above. Clarke was beaten and left on the steps overnight in his tattered clothes. This public humiliation and mistreatment was witnessed by Clarke's comrades including Liam Tobin and Michael Collins, who vowed vengeance, saying Lea-Wilson was a marked man.

The main sorting room in the GPO after the Volunteers abandoned their posts.

The following day the rebels were marched to Richmond Barracks in Inchicore where they awaited court martial. Fifteen of the leaders, including New Ross native Michael O'Hanrahan, were executed at Kilmainham Jail. Roger Casement was hanged in August in Pentonville Jail in London, having failed in an attempt to import arms from Germany. After a number of weeks in detention, many, including Luke Kennedy, were deported to Frangoch Internment Camp in Wales and Knutsford, Wormwood Scrubbs and Wandsworth prisons in England. Among notables held in Frangoch were Arthur Griffith and Michael Collins.

Captain Percival Lea-Wilson settled in Gorey in the years after the Rising, where he was appointed RIC District Inspector. He was based in the RIC barracks, which was later destroyed in an arson attack in 1922 but rebuilt. During his time living in the town he was a member of the local Masonic Lodge and attended Christ Church. He had regular raids carried out in the area in search of arms, making him very unpopular in the town. On one occasion Lea-Wilson set up a cordon of armed RIC men outside Christ Church and blocked a group of Irish Volunteers from Camolin who were returning home from

Michael Collins and Liam Tobin at the Gresham Hotel, January 1922.

a meeting in Gorey. The group included Father Dominic Sweetman, founder of Mount St. Benedict School and a Republican sympathizer. After a heated argument, Lea-Wilson eventually let them pass.

On the morning of 15 June 1920, Percival Lea-Wilson walked to the RIC barracks in Gorey dressed in civilian clothes. He left soon after in the company of Constable Alexander O'Donnell. Lea-Wilson stopped to buy a newspaper at the train station and the pair went their own ways, and Percival read the paper as he strolled towards his home along the Ballycanew Road, shortly before 10am. He paid little heed to a group of men ahead who were standing around a car that had its bonnet raised.

Michael Collins had dispatched IRA volunteers Liam Tobin and Frank Thornton from Dublin, both members of the 'Squad' – Collins' elite unit that executed 'spies and informers'. The operation was sanctioned by IRA General Headquarters and involved a total of ten men: five to scout out the area and five to carry out the shooting. They met with Joe McMahon, Michael McGrath and Michael Sinnott in Enniscorthy and were driven by Jack Whelan in a stolen car to Gorey to carry out the assassination.

As Lea-Wilson approached, the men opened fire and he was struck down by two bullets. He managed to get back on his feet and attempted to run but was caught in a hail of bullets. Lea-Wilson stumbled for a further fifteen yards before collapsing and dying. One of his killers then calmly walked up to the body and fired a final shot to the head to be sure he was really dead. He then casually picked up Lea-Wilson's newspaper from the ground and the killers sped off. A coroner's report later confirmed that he was shot a total of seven times.

Later that evening the news of Lea-Wilson's killing was relayed to Michael Collins, who was in the Wicklow Hotel, a regular haunt of Collins and his 'Squad', on Dublin's Wicklow Street.

He passed the news on to fellow IRA man Joe Sweeney:

"We got the bugger, Joe," announced Collins.

"What are you talking about?" Sweeney asked.

"Do you remember that first night outside the Rotunda – Lea-Wilson?"

"I'll never forget it," Sweeney replied.

"Well," said Collins, "we got him today in Gorey."

The head porter of the Wicklow Hotel, Peter Doran, was shot dead the following January by Collins' men because they believed that he was working as a spy for the British, providing information to Colonel Hill Dillon, the Deputy Chief of British Intelligence in Ireland.

Detail from the Lea-Wilson memorial window by Harry Clarke in Christ Church, Gorey.

Percival's widow, Marie, never believed that her husband had mal-treated the prisoners in 1916 and she had his body returned to England where he was buried with his father in Putney Vale Cemetery, London. A stained-glass window by Harry Clarke was later dedicated to him in Christ Church, Gorey.

THE CARAVAGGIO

In 1924, Marie was on a trip to Edinburgh, where she purchased a large 17th century religious painting that had been hanging in a private house for over a hundred years. It had been sold at auction in Edinburgh in 1921 for £8 and again in 1922 as part of an estate sale and was attributed to the 17th century Dutch artist Gerard van Honthorst (1592-1656) and entitled *The Betrayal of Christ*. The painting depicted Judas betraying Jesus with a kiss and therefore identifying him to the Roman soldiers who were about to take him prisoner. Early in his career Van Honthorst visited Rome and painted in a style influenced by Caravaggio. Marie had the frame restored by James Hicks of Pembroke Street and hung the painting in her house on Fitzwilliam Place.

Marie never remarried and, now in her late 30s, enrolled in Trinity College to study medicine. She graduated in 1928 and the following year became a resident staff member at Sir Patrick Dun's Hospital, which was the teaching hospital for Trinity College. Dr. Marie Lea-Wilson became a consultant in the Children's Hospital, Harcourt Street, where she worked until she died aged 84 in 1971.

Dr Marie Lea-Wilson (née Ryan), widow of the assassinated RIC District Inspector.

While grieving for her dead husband, Marie had gained solace from a priest, Father Thomas Finlay, of the Jesuit Community on Leeson Street. In 1934, she donated the painting that she bought in Edinburgh ten years earlier in trust to the Jesuits and it hung in their dining-room in Leeson Street for over sixty years. In 1990, the 66-inch long dark and dusty old painting was sent to Dublin's National Gallery to be cleaned and restored. The task fell to Sergio Benedetti, an Italian art historian who was then the gallery's senior conservator. Benedetti worked on the painting over the next 18 months and said it was the best copy of a Caravaggio that he had ever seen. Finally, a year later tests established that it was an original and not a copy. Art researchers in Italy found that the painting had been commissioned in 1602 by Ciriaco Mattei, a wealthy and prolific art collector in Rome. In the late 1700s, Caravaggio's name was no longer attributed to the painting and it was inexplicably mislabelled as a work by Van Honthorst. When the Mattei family were selling pieces from the family's vast art collection in the early 1800s, it was purchased by Scottish politician William Nisbet in 1802 in Rome and remained in his home, Archerfield House, Dirleton, until 1921.

Probably the greatest Italian painter of the 17th century, Caravaggio, led a turbulent life. In his book *Lines of Vision*, Wexford native John Banville wrote of Caravaggio: 'What was said of Byron could be as well said of him, that he was mad, bad and dangerous to know, he was dead by the age of 38 from fever, it seems, though he may have been murdered. If it was murder, it is hardly surprising, for he had lived by the sword. Indeed he killed a man himself in 1606.'

The lost Caravaggio had been discussed and sought for many years and versions of *The Taking of Christ* were on exhibition around the world. At a public ceremony in 1993, the baroque masterpiece was

This nameplate once attached to the Caravaggio frame, attributing the painting incorrectly to Van Honthorst. His Italian nickname 'Gherardo delle Notti' was also misspelt and his year of death is also incorrect. He died in 1656.

handed over to the National Gallery of Ireland on indefinite loan. It was presented to the Chairperson of the Gallery's Board, Dr. William Finlay, the grand-nephew of Father Thomas Finlay, to whom Marie Lea-Wilson gave the painting in 1934. The painting is the most prominent exhibit in the gallery and is valued today at over €100 million.

To quote the Jesuit priest Father Noel Barber: 'Had it not been alleged that Percival Lea-Wilson humiliated the Republican prisoners in 1916, he would not have been murdered; had he not been murdered, his wife would not have sought counselling from Fr. Finlay; had she not become Fr. Finlay's client, she would not have given *The Taking of Christ* to the Leeson Street Jesuits; had she not done that, we would not have been able to give the magnificent painting to the National Gallery of Ireland. A strange thread of events.'

Caravaggio's 'The Taking of Christ', missing for 200 years, purchased at auction in 1921 for £8. Marie Lea-Wilson bought it in Edinburgh in 1924 and it is now valued at over €100 million.

Shooting Private Ryan on a Wexford beach

Ballinesker Beach, Curracloe, was transformed into Omaha Beach, Normandy in the summer of 1997. Right: Ballinesker today.

BALLYVALOO BEACH, a couple of miles north of Curracloe, was the first choice of location for the harrowing opening sequence of *Saving Private Ryan*. Close by was the St. John of God convent, which the nuns agreed to make available to the film crew – but not in June 1997. They would have to wait until 15 August as the convent was being used as a retreat centre until then. Director Steven Spielberg was about to find an alternative location, possibly in England, when a Wexford County Council official, over a pint in Asple's Bar on Crescent Quay in Wexford, suggested Ballinesker, a little to the south. Spielberg had found his 'Normandy'.

With a number of blockbusters already under his belt, such as *Jaws, E.T., Jurassic Park* and *Schindler's List,* Steven Spielberg was one of America's most successful filmmakers. As co-founder of Dreamworks Pictures in 1994, he was keen to make the movie of the army private who, because his brothers had been killed in the war, was to be repatriated. It was loosely based on the true story of Frederick Niland, an American soldier of Irish descent whose three brothers, also U.S. soldiers, were believed to have died in the war, though one was ultimately found alive after surviving a Japanese prisoner-of-war camp. Both Spielberg and Tom Hanks were separately captivated by the screenplay by Robert Rodat. Spielberg also considered Harrison Ford and Mel Gibson before choosing Hanks. This was their first collaboration and Hanks was to take the lead role as Captain Miller and Private James Ryan to be played by Matt Damon, who was relatively unknown at the time.

The Normandy beach where D-Day actually occurred has strict filming restrictions and is a place where veterans and descendants silently pay tribute to the troops who lost their lives there. So production designer Tom Sanders visited a variety of alternative beaches in France, England and Ireland before finding Curracloe, which is uncannily similar to the Normandy beaches.

In the summer of 1997, the unspoilt Ballinesker Beach at Curracloe was transformed into Omaha Beach, a 5-mile stretch of the Normandy coast facing the English Channel. Omaha was the code name for one of the five sectors for the Allied invasion of German-occupied France in the Normandy landings on D-Day, 6 June 1944. The Allies had divided the 60-mile coastal stretch chosen for the invasion into five zones codenamed Utah and Omaha (American), Sword and Gold (British) and Juno (Canadian). The landing at Omaha Beach of U.S. troops, who had sailed from South Devon and of whom about 1,000 died, was the opening sequence to be depicted in *Saving Private Ryan*. D-Day was one of the bloodiest battles and the largest amphibious

Ballinesker Beach with 'Rommel's Asparagus' defence, intended as obstacles to tanks and to rip through the bottom of Allied landing craft.

invasion in human history. The operation was the beginning of the liberation of German-occupied France and later Western Europe.

Ballinesker was transformed into a Second World War German stronghold with trails of barbed wire, concrete pillbox bunkers and mini forts erected along the sand dunes, from where the Germans would rain down a relentless barrage of gunfire. The beach was dotted with steel anti-tank obstacles known as 'Belgian gates' and 'Czech hedgehogs'.

The Irish Army Reserve (then known as the FCA) was recommended to Spielberg by Mel Gibson, who had used them in the making of *Braveheart* a couple of years previously. The war epic employed 750 members of the Irish Defence Forces, who were each paid £40 per day as extras, in the opening 20-minute sequence. Many were now movie veterans, having already worked on *Braveheart*. The opening, filmed in Curracloe, cost an extraordinary $12m and was never storyboarded, in order to enhance the realism of the battle. Over twenty disabled extras, mostly amputees, were paid £56 per day. They were fitted with prosthetic limbs, which were blown off under the bombardment of German gunfire. The production team went to great lengths to ensure that the film was as true to life as possible.

Retired U.S. Marine Corps Captain Dale Dye, a Vietnam War veteran who had been a military consultant on many war movies, put the Irish troops through boot camp. 3,000 uniforms, 2,000 pairs of boots and 2,000 replica

Tom Sizemore (Sergeant Horvath) and Tom Hanks (Captain Miller) approaching Ballinesker in the movie.
(photo: Dreamworks Pictures)

Members of the Irish Army Reserve, the FCA, in action on Ballinesker Beach in the opening sequence of Saving Private Ryan. (photo: Dreamworks Pictures)

rifles had to be made and then put through an ageing process. The stunt coordinator was Simon Crane, who had also worked on *Braveheart, Titanic* and many other movies. Most of the landing craft (Higgins boats) were found in Palm Springs, California, refurbished in England and brought into Wexford Harbour prior to filming. There, laden with uniformed troops under the direction of Captain Dye, the vessels were tested on the water and landed on the shingle beach at Ferrybank, where the soldiers rushed ashore to engage the enemy, much to the delight of locals watching from Wexford Bridge.

Spielberg depicted the Omaha Beach landing as it really happened in 1944. "Omaha Beach was a slaughter", he stressed. "It was a complete foul-up, from the expeditionary forces, to the reconnaissance forces, to the saturation bombing that missed most of its primary targets. Given that, I didn't want to glamourize what had really happened, so I tried to be as brutally honest as I could." On shooting the opening sequence at Curracloe, Tom Hanks said: "The adrenaline rush was like nothing I had ever experienced on any other movie...There's terror in our eyes in some of those scenes, and rightly so, because we were genuinely scared though we knew that it was all fake."

While the location of the film represented German-occupied Normandy, ten acres of land used at Ballinesker had actually been occupied by a German native up to 1960. It was then sold to local man Denis Cloney, who was now renting it out to the production company.

The Wexford Film Commission, who secured the movie coming to the county, was formed in 1993 with a £20,000 investment, which was quickly matched by the County Council and private sector. By the time filming had ended, the local economy had benefited by about £4m. It is estimated that £1.25 million was spent on accommodation, £300,000 on direct labour, £270,000 on transport and fuel, £1.5 million on location and construction costs and £650,000 on the Irish Army, FCA and Navy as extras.

The Defence Forces were housed in St. Peter's College in Wexford, where the former dormitories were revamped and showers installed at a cost of £40,000, paid for by Dreamworks. Most of the actors stayed in hotels such as Kelly's in Rosslare Strand, the Devereux in Rosslare Harbour and the Ferrycarrig Hotel, from where they were collected each morning at 6.30am, on the set for 7am and shooting began at 8.30am. Tom Hanks and Steven

Tom Hanks and his unit on reconnaissance following the 'Normandy' landing, filmed at Tottenham Green outside Taghmon.

Spielberg, along with their wives, ten children and two babysitters, had taken nine rooms in the luxury Marlfield House Hotel just outside Gorey. The soldiers often started at 5am and put in a 14-hour day.

Filming began in June 1997 and lasted for 25 days. The first two weeks saw torrential rain but for the filming of the D-Day landing the weather was perfect for Spielberg; cloudy with showers, just like it was 50 years earlier in Normandy. On the third day of filming, up to twenty uniformed extras were suffering from hypothermia and were admitted to Wexford Hospital, where they got some respite. Another extra, FCA soldier Graham Smith, was sleeping on a grassy area close to the beach in soft sand during a break in filming. An army jeep drove over his legs and he suffered severe bruising. He had to use crutches for about six weeks after the accident and was awarded £10,000 at Wexford Circuit Court two years later.

Hundreds of visitors flocked to Curracloe, on the longest stretch of beach in Ireland, to catch a glimpse of the battle scenes from a distance. The filmset was strictly out of bounds, especially to photographers. The Irish Naval Service ship *LÉ Orla* was deployed to prevent trawlers and leisure craft from entering the sea area off Ballinesker during filming. Wexford was on a bit of a high, with roads festooned with the county colours of purple and gold. Midway through filming, the Wexford senior hurling team defeated their old rivals Kilkenny, 2–14 to 1–11, in the Leinster Final.

"It was a magic time filming in Wexford," recalled Tom Hanks with affection in a recent interview in 2019. He recalled, after three weeks of filming, asking if he could see some of the footage. He was told that he could watch it in a little hall in nearby Screen. Waiting in a car for somebody to arrive to open up, a young lad out walking stopped and asked: "Are ya in de film?" "Yes I am", Hanks replied, and the boy continued on his way.

Actor Tom Sizemore, who played Sergeant Horvath, was a heroin addict prior to filming the movie. Spielberg forced him to take drug tests on set and, according to Sizemore, Spielberg "said he would fire me on the spot and shoot all 58 days that I'd worked over again with someone else."

One actor who played the part of a U.S. soldier on the beach was Dublin-born actor Andrew Scott, now widely known for his role as Moriarty in the BBC's *Sherlock* television series, for which he won a BAFTA award. He recalled his time in Curracloe in 1997: "Filming it, you couldn't see the camera, you

Matt Damon, who played Private James Ryan, was relatively unknown when cast by Spielberg. But shortly before filming, he won his first Oscar for Best Actor in 'Good Will Hunting'. (photo: Dreamworks Pictures)

couldn't see Spielberg, and you had no idea of the camerawork. You had no idea where they were. It was just you heard, 'Action!', and you had the sound of explosions, had dirt flying in your face, and you couldn't really see anything. You kind of knew that, when it was edited together, that it was going to be extraordinary, though. It was an amazing experience."

When filming of the landing was complete, Spielberg now wanted to shoot several scenes in which Captain Miller's unit are on reconnaissance through the battle-scarred Normandy countryside. A suitable field in the Curracloe area was chosen but the landowner was looking for £12,000 from the production company for one day's shooting. Despite efforts by the Wexford Film Commission and Wexford County Council to have the price reduced, agreement was not reached. The production team instead settled on a location that they had already surveyed in Tottenham Green, a mile outside Taghmon. On 16 July, the entire production team moved lock, stock and barrel to Taghmon. The huge convoy passed through the village early that evening, totally unexpectedly and to the amazement of local villagers, and were directed into a field owned by local farmer Jim Parle.

When the film crew left Ireland in July, they relocated to an abandoned British Aerospace facility in Hartfield, north of London. Tom Sanders and his team reconstructed a bombed-out French village next to the site, and even dug out a section of river, complete with bridge, for the final scene.

Aware that the opening scene filmed in Wexford would shock and upset audiences, Spielberg, Hanks and Damon went on nationwide publicity tours across America to warn audiences what to expect and to explain why the brutality was necessary. In preparation for the film's release, the U.S. Department of Veterans Affairs established a special hotline for members to call. When the movie opened in cinemas in the USA, some D-Day veterans walked out halfway through while some were reported to have sought counselling, having seen the slaughter on the big screen.

Time magazine described the opening scenes as 'the greatest combat sequence ever made'. *Screen International* went with the headline 'Spielberg's most terrifying rollercoaster ride' and it was ranked number one on *TV Guide*'s list of the '50 Greatest Movie Moments'. *Empire* magazine said the beach landing was 'the best battle scene of all time'. The film, which had a budget of $70m, grossed over $73m in just the first 10 days in cinemas across the USA and eventually grossed a total of $482m worldwide. It went on to win five Oscars in 1999, including the gong for Best Director for Steven Spielberg. It also won Best Cinematography, Best Sound, Best Film Editing and Best Sound Effects Editing.

The production team spent four weeks cleaning up the Ballinsker Beach area and brought it back to its original state, as had been agreed beforehand with Wexford County Council. The guns were now silent and the troops had gone, and life returned to normal around Wexford and Curracloe.

Legendary American civil rights campaigner in Wexford

Fugitive slave and social reformer, Frederick Douglass (1818-1895), gave public lectures across Ireland, including Wexford's Assembly Rooms, in 1845.

FREDERICK DOUGLASS, the escaped slave and abolitionist, visited Ireland in 1845 and stayed for four months as part of an almost two-year lecture tour of Britain and Ireland. The renowned orator gave talks over two nights in the Assembly Rooms (now Wexford Arts Centre) and in Dublin forged a great friendship with the liberator, Daniel O'Connell. He was shocked at the poverty he encountered in Ireland, a country on the brink of famine.

Born into slavery as Frederick Bailey in Maryland in a log cabin on the rural Eastern Shore of Chesapeake Bay in 1818, he lived with his grandparents, Isaac and Betsey Bailey, until he was taken to work on a plantation where his mother had been a slave. His father was a white man, possibly his 'owner' Aaron Anthony, and his mother was Harriet Bailey, who lived some miles away on one of Anthony's farms. Anthony was an estate manager on the plantation and owned about thirty slaves. The estate formed part of the vast 9,000-acre Wye Plantation of Colonel Edward Lloyd, former Governor of Maryland, who owned 180 slaves. The Lloyd family built a substantial fortune through the African slave trade and the cultivation of tobacco. The number of slaves in their service reached a staggering 700 individuals over the next twenty years.

When Frederick was six years old, he was taken by his grandmother to work as a domestic servant in Anthony's stone cottage on the Wye Plantation. There he met his older brother Perry and sisters Sarah and Eliza, whom he hardly knew. His grandmother Betsey slipped away without saying goodbye, thinking it best for the little boy. That night, Frederick cried himself to sleep on a cold, stone floor.

Frederick witnessed many beatings by Aaron Anthony of his slaves. His first sighting was the violent abuse of his 15-year-old aunt Hester. She had refused her owner's predatory advances and when he discovered that she had been out one night with one of the Lloyd slaves, a boy her own age, he stripped her naked and whipped her until blood dripped down to the floor. Frederick would witness many more beatings by his owner.

Also living in the cottage was Aaron Anthony's married daughter Lucretia. She was about 20 years old and married to Thomas Auld, a captain on Lloyd's ship, the *Sally Lloyd*. 'Miss Lucretia', as Frederick called her, was kind to the young boy and often sneaked him pieces of bread when no one was looking. Perhaps she had heard the whispers that Frederick was her half-brother. By this time his mother Harriet was dead.

Frederick was eight when Lucretia arranged for him to be moved to her brother-in-law, Hugh Auld and his wife Sophia in the great shipbuilding

Black men, women and children were used as slave labour on the cotton plantations in the southern states until slavery was abolished in 1865, following the American Civil War.

city of Baltimore on the far shore of Chesapeake Bay. Still a slave and the property of Aaron Anthony, he was warmly welcomed by 'Miss Sopha,' who treated him as she did her own son Tommy. Frederick ran errands for Hugh Auld, his new master, a carpenter who was trying to set up his own shipbuilding business. Sophia was a Methodist and would read the Bible aloud in the house. This awoke a curiosity in Frederick. He asked her to teach him how to read, which she readily did. They would read passages from the Bible slowly together and Frederick was quick to learn. But her husband put a stop to this, saying "Learning would spoil the best nigger in the world." But Frederick would continue to read in secret and also taught himself how to write.

Following the death of Aaron Anthony, his slaves were to be divided between his two sons and Thomas Auld. Now nine years old, Frederick had to return to one of Anthony's farms in 1827, where his thirty slaves were lined up, inspected and valued by two lawyers. Douglass later wrote: "Men and women, young and old, married and single; moral and intellectual beings, in open contempt of their humanity, levelled at a blow with horses, sheep, horned cattle, and swine…and all subjected to the same narrow inspection, to ascertain their value in gold and silver – the only standard of worth applied by slaveholders to slaves! How vividly at that moment did the brutalizing power of slavery flash before me!"

The greatest fear of the slaves was to be separated from their families by being sold south to the expanding cotton plantations of the new slave states like Alabama and Mississippi. This was the fate of Frederick's sister Sarah but Frederick was assigned back to Thomas Auld, whose wife Lucretia had by now passed away. Auld sent him straight back to his brother Hugh Auld in Baltimore, where he was warmly welcomed on his return by 'Miss Sopha'.

Between 1810 and 1820, Maryland exported 124,000 slaves southwards, answering southern slave buyers' insatiable appetite for black workers for their rapidly-growing cotton industry and their cry of "Cash! Cash, for Negroes!" It suited some slave owners in the region, where there was a steady decline in labour-intensive tobacco farming. For economic reasons, many surplus slaves were being granted freedom and these, usually older men, ended up in cities like Baltimore – the 'black capital of America'. Frederick spent the next five years in Baltimore, where slaves and free blacks mixed

Advertising 'Negro sales' in Atlanta, Georgia in 1864, a year before the abolition of slavery.

reasonably freely with immigrants from Europe, including the many Irish.

At the age of twelve Douglass purchased his very first book: a second-hand copy of *The Columbian Orator*. He paid fifty cents for it with money he secretly earned from shoe-shining. The book included a collection of many famous speeches that promoted patriotism and republicanism. The speeches, which included contributions by George Washington, Napoleon Bonaparte and the like, were learned in schools by boys wishing to enter public-speaking competitions. Frederick kept his book hidden in the loft of the house but would secretly read the speeches over and over. He learned the importance of pronunciation and the effective use of gestures in public speaking, which featured in the book's introduction. Included was the celebrated speech in the Irish House of Commons in 1795 in support of Catholic emancipation by Arthur O'Connor, who later joined the United Irishmen. Words like 'liberty', 'freedom' and 'equality' would make a deep impression on the young boy – as well as 'abolition', which also featured in the book as an imagined dialogue between a master and his slave.

Frederick was 15 when he was sent back to Thomas Auld, who in turn passed him on to a farm run by a certain Edward Covey, known to be a 'Negro breaker'. Unfamiliar with farm work, he was whipped every week for six months and the constant punishment wore him down. Following an attack on his master, Auld had him hired out for a year to an older farmer, William Freeland, whom he later described as 'the best master I ever had, until I became my own master.' After a failed escape plan in 1836 when he was 17, Auld sent Frederick back to work in the shipyards of Baltimore.

As the years passed, slaves in the city were allowed to hire themselves out. Frederick could now find his own work and collect wages so long as he paid Auld $3 a week. Still a slave, he found his own lodgings and mixed with free slaves. He got engaged to a free black woman, Anna Murray. He was 20 years old when he finally succeeded in boarding a train heading north to the slave state of Delaware. He was dressed in seaman's clothes and carrying forged sailor's free papers and managed to reach the free state city of New York. Anna joined him a few days later and they were soon married. However, New York was not a safe place to be, with slave-catchers scouring the streets for runaways. The newly-weds moved on into Massachusetts where Frederick changed his surname to Douglass.

Working as a labourer on the docks in New Bedford, he soon began to speak at local anti-slave group meetings and delivered his first public speech to the Massachusetts Anti-Slavery Society. Douglass was offered a position as a paid agent for the society to go on the road to tell his story of his life as a slave. His speeches were picked up by *The Liberator*, a radical abolitionist newspaper. Frederick was now reading Shakespeare and his speeches were powerful and eloquent. 'People doubted if I had ever been a slave. They said I did not talk like a slave, look like a slave, nor act like a slave,' he later wrote.

In the summer of 1845, his book *Narrative of the Life of Frederick Douglass* was published and became an immediate bestseller. It would go on to become an American literature classic. It was highly praised in the Northern press but denounced in the slave states as a 'catalogue of lies'. In fear of Frederick now being recaptured by his owner Thomas Auld in Maryland, the Massachusetts abolitionists decided to send him on a two-year-long speaking and fundraising tour of the United Kingdom.

His first stop was Ireland, where his *Narrative* was published by Richard Webb, the Dublin Quaker printer and founding member of the Hibernian Anti-Slavery Association. The Quakers in Ireland were strong advocates of abolition. Webb was responsible for setting up his speaking engagements around the country.

The 27-year-old Douglass sailed out of Boston in August 1845 on the new Cunard Line wooden paddle-steamer, the *Cambria*, on the twelve-day voyage, stopping first in Liverpool. He was accompanied by James Buffum, a white abolitionist from Massachusetts. Although he had a first-class ticket, he was relegated to steerage on account of his colour. On the journey he sold some copies of his book and was invited by the captain to deliver a speech to the passengers. This turned into a brawl, however, with some hecklers calling him a liar and shouts of 'down with the nigger' and threats to 'throw the damned nigger overboard'. Douglass gave up and disappeared back down below decks. Having arrived in Liverpool, Douglass and Buffum sailed two days later, again on the *Cambria*, to Dublin, where they remained for six weeks.

Dublin had lost much of its late 18th century grandeur and was a city in decline. He was taken on a city tour and visited Dalkey and Howth before witnessing the extreme poverty in the city. 'The streets were…alive with beggars displaying the greatest wretchedness,' he later wrote.

He delivered his first anti-slavery lectures in the Royal Exchange on Dame Street (the present-day City Hall) and the Friends [Quaker] Meeting House in nearby Eustace Street to capacity crowds. He made an immediate impact and was praised in the Dublin newspapers for his 'cultivated mind'. Of his time in Dublin, he remarked that 'one of the most pleasing features of my visit…has been a total absence of…prejudice against me on account of my colour.' He continued his lecture tours with three successive appearances in the Music Hall (later the Abbey Theatre).

Frederick's first encounter with Daniel O'Connell was on Carlisle Bridge (now known as O'Connell Bridge). He later went to hear the great liberator speak in the Conciliation Hall on Burgh Quay (later the Irish Press offices), where he denounced slavery, not knowing that Douglass was present in the hall. Buffum amicably pushed Douglass onto the stage and O'Connell introduced him as 'the black O'Connell of the United States'.

On a visit later to Cork, Frederick Douglass was introduced in the Cork Temperance Institute by the teetotalist, Father Theobald Mathew. Douglass signed the pledge to abstain from drinking alcohol, but a few years later, on a visit to the United States, Father Mathew found himself at the centre of the abolitionist debate. The Catholic Archbishop of New York, John Hughes, was an anti-abolitionist and wanted assurances from Mathew that he would not stray outside his remit of battling alcohol consumption. Mathew snubbed an invitation to publicly condemn slavery and defended his position by pointing out that there was nothing in the scriptures that prohibited it. Douglass felt 'grieved, humbled and mortified' and 'wondered how being a Catholic priest should inhibit him from denouncing the sin of slavery as much as the sin of intemperance.'

Richard Webb's grandmother had lived in Wexford and it seemed a natural first destination outside Dublin. In October 1845, Douglass made the ten-hour road journey from Dublin to Wexford, taking the daily coach at 7am from Dawson Street. He was accompanied by James Buffum and Richard Webb, whose son Alfred would later recall 'the delightful, entrancing, narrow streets of Wexford, where from the coach-roof at a few points in the Main Street one could shake hands...with people in the windows on both sides and where house after house was occupied by Friends [Quakers] carrying on different businesses and selling behind their own counters.' Quaker numbers had grown steadily across Wexford, with meeting houses built in Crossabeg, Camolin, Ferns, Taghmon, Enniscorthy and Wexford town. In 1842, a new meeting house was completed at the bottom of High Street, replacing an earlier one erected in 1746. The house fell into disuse in 1927.

Sign on the old Quaker meeting house on High Street, Wexford.

Douglass, Buffum and Webb stayed with Joseph Poole, a cousin of Webb's in Growtown near Taghmon. Douglass spoke on two successive nights in the Assembly Rooms' meeting room upstairs in the Market House in Cornmarket, on Tuesday 7 and Wednesday 8 October. In the early 20th century the building, constructed in 1775, became the headquarters of Wexford Corporation and was known as the Town Hall. There was a large ballroom and supper-room located on the first floor. The Corporation moved to the Tate School at Windmill Hill in 1949, when it became the Municipal Buildings. In 1974, the 200-year-old Market House became Wexford Arts Centre.

Tickets for the lectures were advertised as on sale at the door for 4 pence and the audience was largely from the Quaker community. Copies of the Richard Webb edition of Douglass's *Narrative* were on sale on the night. Joseph Poole, Webb's cousin, reported on the lectures in the *Wexford Independent* a few days after the talks and wrote:

'Will you through the medium of your paper help forward the good cause by

The Market House and Assembly Rooms (built in 1775) in Cornmarket, Wexford, where Douglass gave two public lectures in 1845, is now Wexford Arts Centre. Photographed in 1904 by Robert French. (National Library of Ireland)

making known the feeling of a large assembly of your fellow townsmen, expressed in the following resolution which passed the meeting without a single dissenting voice. Proposed by Joseph Poole; seconded by William Whitney: Resolved – That we have listened with interest to the development of the horrors of American slaveholding in the United States, by Frederick Douglass (recently a slave in that country) and that we are filled with the greatest disgust and loathing at the horrible inconsistency between the profession and practice of those who – calling themselves Christians, Republicans and Democrats, hold men, women and children in the most degrading bondage, and we hereby register our remonstrance against all such, and declare, that as lovers of liberty – as Irishmen having human hearts and human sympathies, we utter our solemn conviction, that no Slaveholder can be Christian any more than Pirates and Robbers can be honest men; and we hereby repudiate all such as the enemies of the human race and the rights of man.'

The *Wexford Conservative* published a piece submitted by an anonymous contributor who had attended one of the lectures. He retold an anecdote that the light-skinned Douglass related on the night. While travelling by coach through the northern state of Vermont one night, he chatted cordially with two white Americans. 'As soon as the light broke in upon them, one of the gentlemen peeped under the hat of Douglass, then suddenly throwing himself back, he stirred his companion and whispered to him, "By God, it's a nigger!". The two men were prejudiced against the tincture of the poor creole's skin. Had they turned their eyes upon their own…hearts, they would have seen real blackness in them, not superficially, but throughout all their recesses.'

Frederick Douglass with his second wife Helen Pitts (sitting) and her sister Eva. Their interracial marriage in 1884 caused a storm in America.

These newspaper reports were finding their way into the American papers and affecting public opinion there. From Wexford, Frederick Douglass and his colleagues continued on to Waterford and spoke in the City Hall on 9 October. In advance of his arrival in the city, the *Chronicle and Munster Advertiser* claimed that 'almost every shabby and eliminated Irishman, immediately that he leaves his own bog and potatoes, becomes a most ardent admirer of this nasty "institution".' The *Boston Pilot*, the leading Irish American newspaper at the time, took offence and insisted that the Irish in America hated 'slavery and tyranny' and the reality of slavery was not as bad as portrayed in the Irish and British press.

Douglass continued on to Cork, Limerick and finally Belfast. He left Ireland briefly and travelled to Birmingham, where he gave a talk at the invitation of John Cadbury, a Quaker and founder of the vast chocolate empire. He finally left the 'Emerald Isle', as he liked to call it, in early 1846 for a year-long lecture tour of Britain. After only eleven days in Ireland, he wrote: 'Instead of the bright blue sky of America, I am covered with the soft grey fog of the Emerald Isle. I breathe, and lo! the chattel becomes a man.' Reflecting on his time in Ireland he wrote: 'I seem to have undergone a transformation. I live a new life.'

While Douglass was in England, a group of anti-slavery campaigners in Newcastle raised £150 and sent it to the Auld family back in Maryland, the price they required for his release from slavery. When he returned to America in April 1847, he was now an international celebrity. He moved his family to Rochester in upstate New York and started his own newspaper, the *North Star*, and a few years later, *Frederick Douglass's Paper*, in which he relentlessly attacked slavery. During the American Civil War (1861 to 1865), he advised Abraham Lincoln in the White House and succeeded in convincing him to enlist African-Americans into the army and that the abolition of slavery should be a goal of the war. Slavery was finally abolished in the United States in 1865.

While Frederick Douglass also spoke on temperance, women's rights, the abolition of capital punishment and land reform, his visit coincided with the first signs of an unknown potato blight. It originated on the east coast of the United States in 1843 and had reached France and the Low Countries by summer 1845, and Ireland in September of that year. The Great Famine lasted four years and claimed about a million lives. Nearly two million Irish people emigrated, the majority to the United States.

This plaque on the exterior of Wexford Arts Centre was unveiled in 2019 to commemorate the visit of the 19th century's most influential African American.

Driven to insanity after a
visit from the Devil

THE LEGEND of the ghost of Anne Tottenham of Loftus Hall has lived on for over 250 years. Known as Redmond Hall since the 1350s, it became the home of the Loftus family in 1666 when it was renamed Loftus Hall. A somewhat ominous date, containing as it does 666, 'the number of the Beast'. The current mansion is known as 'the most haunted house in Ireland.'

Charles Tottenham (1685-1758) of Tottenham Green, near Horetown, married Ellinor Cliffe in 1712. Their son Charles Tottenham (1716-95) married Anne Loftus and they had six children, including another Anne, born in 1744. Charles and Anne resided with their daughter in Loftus Hall.

The story goes that one stormy winter's night in about 1760, a ship was forced to take shelter at nearby Slade harbour. A young passenger on horseback rode through the storm seeking shelter and was drawn towards lights coming from the windows of Loftus Hall, one of the few houses on wind-swept Hook Peninsula. The stranger began knocking on the outer gate and Charles Tottenham welcomed the handsome young gentleman, who was dressed entirely in black, into the house, where he stayed for a number of days. He proved himself 'an agreeable companion and a finished gentleman', according to an account of the episode written by Rev. George Reade that appeared in *The Whitehall Review* in 1882. Rev. Reade was a colleague of the Bishop of Clogher, the Rt. Rev. Robert Tottenham, a brother of Charles Tottenham.

The family played cards with the visitor in the evenings. In those times it was not considered respectable for a girl to play cards, but Anne insisted on joining them. With Anne as his partner, their guest invariably won. Anne was falling in love with the young man but her parents did not approve. During a card game, when Anne dropped a card on the floor and bent to pick it up, she screamed when she spotted that, instead of a foot, the visitor had a cloven hoof. Anne screeched hysterically and the stranger 'vanished in a thunderclap, leaving a brimstone smell behind.' He had exited through the ceiling and according to tradition the hole in the plasterwork could never be repaired. The family believed that the guest was the Devil in disguise.

Anne went into deep shock and subsequently refused food and drink. She fell into a state of insanity and remained in the Tapestry room for the rest of her life. She became an embarrassment to her family and was kept locked away in the room, where she remained sitting in a hunched position at the window for fear that she might miss the return of the stranger. By the time she died on 1 November 1775, aged 31, her bones had fused together in that hunched position and a special coffin had to be made for her corpse. This was confirmed in the 1940s when the Tottenham crypt was opened and the unusually-shaped coffin was seen.

Following Anne's death, there were frequent reports of noises and poltergeist activity in the house that upset the servants. The Tottenham and Loftus families were Protestant, and engaged a number of Protestant clergymen to try to put a stop to this but they all failed. Eventually they sent for the local Catholic priest, Fr. Thomas Broaders, who was parish priest of the united parishes of the Hook and Ramsgrange. He was also a tenant on the Loftus estate and was asked to exorcise the house. He performed a lengthy exorcism and

The 1st Marquess of Ely, another Charles Tottenham, was the first cousin of Anne, who was said to have been visited by the Devil in Loftus Hall.

succeeded in confining the activity of the evil spirit to the Tapestry room. In appreciation, the Loftus family leased several townlands within the estate to Father Broaders, who had them occupied by his parishioners. This was a very unusual arrangement in the country in the late eighteenth century when Catholicism was still technically illegal. In addition, he was permitted to build churches at Poulfur and Templetown. Father Broaders is buried in Horetown Cemetery and this rhyme relates to his burial site: *'Here lies the body of Thomas Broaders, who did good and prayed for all and banished the Devil from Loftus Hall.'*

But the ghostly appearance of a young woman, presumably Anne Tottenham, along with poltergeist activity continued in Loftus Hall, most frequently in the Tapestry room. In 1790, the father of Rev. George Reade was staying with friends in the Hall and was given the Tapestry room to sleep in. 'Something heavy leapt upon his bed, growling like a dog. The curtains were torn back and the clothes stripped from the bed', wrote Rev. Reade. Suspecting that 'some of his companions were playing tricks', he shouted out at them and fired his pistol up the chimney to frighten them off. But he searched the room and found nothing and the door had remained locked, just as he had left it before getting into bed.

Another Charles Tottenham, a first cousin of Anne Tottenham, assumed the surname of Loftus in 1783 when he inherited the estates of his uncle Henry Loftus. The title Marquess of Ely was created later for him in 1800.

Charles Tottenham Loftus was succeeded by his son John Loftus, 2nd Marquess of Ely, upon his death in 1806. His valet, Shannon, was given the

The old Loftus Hall where Anne Tottenham Loftus lived in the mid-1700s. A Norman castle, built by Redmond FitzGerald, originally stood on the site. This was replaced in about 1350 with Redmond Hall and the Loftus Hall that we see today was constructed in 1872.

Tapestry room and one night he woke the entire household with his screams. He related how the bed curtains had been violently torn back and he saw 'a tall lady dressed in stiff brocaded silk.' Shannon fled the house in terror.

On another occasion, George Reade and his father were both staying in Loftus Hall. Unaware of his father's earlier experience, George chose to sleep in the Tapestry room. One night while he was sitting up in bed reading, the door opened and a tall lady in a stiff dress passed silently through the room to a closet in the corner, where she disappeared. On another night he had the same experience as his father:

A young John Henry Loftus, the 4th Marquess of Ely and grand-nephew of Anne Tottenham, with his mother Jane, c.1860. John later had the present-day Loftus Hall rebuilt between 1872-84.
(National Portrait Gallery London)

something heavy jumping on the bed, growling, and tearing off the bedclothes. He leapt out of bed, lit a candle, but could find nothing. He made inquiries and spoke with an old local woman named Haggard, who lived to the age of 106. She had told him the whole story, and remembered Father Broaders.

In 1857, John Henry Loftus became the 4th Marquess, at the age of 8. By 1868, he had made many alterations to the house and the Tapestry room was now the Billiards room. Reade once more visited the Hall and asked the old housekeeper how 'Miss Anne' had taken to these changes. She replied: 'Oh Master George, don't talk about her. Last night she made a horrid noise knocking the billiard balls about!'

When John Henry Loftus came of age, he undertook, with his mother's guidance, an extensive rebuilding of Loftus Hall between 1872 and 1884, with no expense spared. He married Caroline Caithness in 1875 but they had no children. Some believe that the old Hall was entirely demolished and rebuilt, while some experts believe that some elements of the former house were retained and it was built on the foundations of the earlier 17th century house. Some of the features in the new Loftus Hall had not been seen in houses in Ireland at the time, such as flushing toilets and blown-air heating. The new house featured a magnificent hand-carved Jacobean style oak staircase, an ornate mosaic tile floor and elaborate parquet flooring. Much of the inspiration was taken from Osborne House on the Isle of Wight, the holiday residence of Queen Victoria.

The mother of John Henry Loftus was Lady Jane (née Hope-Vere). She was Lady of the Bedchamber to Queen Victoria from 1851 to 1889 and very close to the queen. The family hoped that one day Queen Victoria would visit the new Loftus Hall, which was now a mansion fit for a queen, but it wasn't to be. Towards the end of 1860, Jane related the ghost story and several alleged apparitions in the old Loftus Hall to Queen Victoria. Her Majesty said she did not believe in such things but that her husband, Prince Albert, did and he should not be told.

Jane's husband, James Loftus, had died in 1857 aged 43 on the shore next to Loftus Hall. She had many suitors following the tragedy but never remarried. She became one of the Queen's most trusted and hard-working attendants and her health suffered as a result. Jane resigned on the death of her only son John Henry, aged only 39, in 1889 and died herself the following year. She is buried beside her husband in Kensal Green Cemetery, London.

John's wife Caroline lived until 1917 and the Loftus estate, now diminished financially, was left to John's cousin who eventually put it up for sale. It was purchased by the Sisters of Providence in 1917, who turned it into a convent and a school for young girls interested in joining the order. In 1936, it was acquired by the Rosminian Order of nuns until it was sold in 1983 to Michael Devereux, who ran it as the 'Loftus Hall Hotel' until 1991. The mansion stood empty for a number of years until 2011 when the current owners, the Quigley family, bought it. They have taken advantage of its troubled past and now provide ghost tours of the house: 'The most haunted house in Ireland'.

Tottenham Green, near Horetown, which was the original home of Charles Tottenham, was built in the reign of Queen Elizabeth I. It was bought by Michael Neale of Ballymitty in 1945, who had also purchased Great Saltee Island two years earlier, giving himself the title 'Prince of the Saltee Islands.' Neale had the house demolished around 1950 after it had stood for nearly 400 years.

Final voyage of the dredger 'Portláirge' to Saltmills

The old steam dredger lies forlorn near Saltmills on the shore of Bannow Bay. (photo: Des Kiely)

BUILT IN 1907, before the *Titanic,* by the Liffey Dockyards in Dublin, the dredger *Portláirge* operated in the port of Waterford, excavating mud from the bed of the River Suir for 75 years. It has been lying in shallow water in Bannow Bay at St. Kearns near Saltmills for over 30 years. Local man Seán Finn had bought it in 1987 with the intention of 'doing something with it' but says he 'never got around to it'.

For most of the twentieth century the *Portláirge* was an iconic part of the city of Waterford. The grab hopper dredger was built for the Waterford Harbour Commissioners and launched towards the end of 1907. The shipping magazine *Syren & Shipping* reported at the time: '*On taking delivery of the vessel, Mr. Allingham, Secretary of the Waterford Harbour Commissioners, and Mr. Friel, harbour engineer, under whose superintendence the vessel had been built, expressed themselves thoroughly satisfied in the vessel and all its details and in the manner in which the contract had been carried out.*'

The *Portláirge* dredged the mud banks along the Waterford Quays, keeping them clear for ships to load and unload their cargoes. On board was a crew of

The Portláirge at work at Waterford Quay. The clam-shell buckets dredged mud from the river bed for 75 years.

seven: the captain, an engineer, a stoker to keep the coal fire burning, two crane drivers and two deckhands. The vessel could travel at a speed of 6 or 7 knots per hour. It had a capacity to carry 500 tons of mud removed from the bed of the river and would release the material at the mouth of the Suir estuary, between Dunmore East and the Hook Peninsula. But there were local anecdotes that, with the turning tide, the mud would sometimes return to the quays before the dredger. Powered by coal and steam, the *Portláirge* was the last working steamship in Ireland and the last remaining such vessel in the world. After 75 years, the old twin-engine dredger broke down in December 1982.

Waterford Harbour Commissioners had plans to sell it to Maryport Maritime Museum in Cumbria in the north of England, overlooking the Solway Firth to the Scottish coast, but the deal fell through. The dredger remained berthed at Scotch Quay in Waterford for five years and there was local opposition to it being sold for scrap. Eventually it was purchased by Seán Finn of Saltmills in 1987 for £3,000.

This stencil artwork 'Deep Love' was painted on the hull by the Dublin street artist known as ADW.

On 26 August 1987, the historic dredger left Waterford for the last time and sailed under its own steam downriver into Waterford Harbour, around Hook Head and into the shallow waters of Bannow Bay, where it beached near St. Kearns, just beyond Saltmills. On

The rusted stern of the old steam dredger, now anchored in Bannow Bay at St. Kearns near Saltmills. (photo: Des Kiely)

board were its new owner, Seán Finn, a mechanic from New Ross, the dredger's former fireman and a priest who was a steam enthusiast. The following week, the *Waterford News & Star* quoted Finn as saying: 'There will be more voyages in the future, the ship is a fine example of Irish workmanship and I am glad she did not go abroad.' But the vessel that once carried mud from the port of Waterford now ironically sits in the mud of Bannow Bay. The port authorities in Waterford have expressed some interest in bringing the historic dredger home again and renovating it.

SALTMILLS

The village was established in 1814 by Caesar Colclough of nearby Tintern Abbey. Cistercian monks lived at Tintern for 300 years before it was suppressed in 1536. The estate was granted to Anthony Colclough from Staffordshire, a member of King Henry VIII's army in Ireland. The village of Tintern had grown up south of the abbey but John Colclough, who developed the walled gardens, wanted to remove the hamlet from the grounds and relocate it out of sight of the abbey. But after John was killed in the infamous duel with William Alcock of Wilton Castle, Bree in 1807, his brother Caesar created the new settlement in 1814. As their leases expired, the tenants of Tintern were moved to the adjoining townland of Saltmills and the old village of Tintern was eventually demolished. The hump-backed Tintern Bridge was constructed, providing access across the Ban River on one of the main routes between Wellingtonbridge to Fethard-on-Sea and the Hook.

The Colclough family were benevolent landlords, held in high regard by their tenants. An earlier Caesar Colclough, who died in 1766, even had his own hurling team. It is said that when he took them to play in Cornwall, the team earned the nickname 'yellow bellies' because of the yellow sashes that they wore. The name is still used today with reference to the county team.

The name Saltmills comes from a tide-mill that once stood here and was driven by the tidal rise and fall of Bannow Bay. A dam with a sluice would have been created across the estuary of the River Ban that flows through the Tintern estate, to create a reservoir. As the tide came in, it entered the mill-pond through a one-way gate. This gate closed automatically when the tide began to fall. When the tide was low enough, the stored water could be released to turn the water-wheel that operated the mill.

From *A Topographical Dictionary of Ireland* by Samuel Lewis, published in 1837: *SALT-MILLS, a village, in the parish of TINTERN, barony of SHELBURNE, county of WEXFORD, and province of LEINSTER, 2½ miles (N.) from Fethard; containing 206 inhabitants. The village of Tintern, which was contiguous to the abbey of that name, the property of Cæsar Colclough, Esq., was taken down within the last 20 years, and rebuilt upon the townland of Salt Mills, by which name it is now more generally known. It is situated on the western side of an inlet of the sea, called Bannow bay, and in 1831 contained 29 houses and cottages, all neatly white-washed, and several of them painted and ornamented in front with small gardens. The female inhabitants are mostly employed in straw-platting and bonnet-making, which are carried on to some extent; and some of the males are employed in fishing. A school for boys and a dispensary are entirely supported by Mr. Colclough.*

Tintern Bridge and river estuary at Saltmills. (photo: Des Kiely)

ST. KEARNS

One hundred years ago, on 12 October 1920, at the height of the War of Independence that resulted in the deaths of 2,000 people, five men were killed and nine others injured in an explosion in St. Kearns, a short distance from Saltmills. It was the greatest number of casualties in County Wexford during the war that began after Ireland declared independence from Britain and a provisional government, Dáil Éireann, was formed in January 1919. A truce was finally agreed in July 1921.

Monument erected in memory of the men killed at St. Kearns in 1920. It was the greatest single loss of Republican lives in Wexford since 1798.

Explosives were being prepared by 14 members of the South Wexford Brigade of the IRA in an old unoccupied house in St. Kearns on that fateful night. According to the Military Archives, Michael Conway, a Volunteer from Curraghmore, Ballycullane, stated: 'Another Volunteer was also engaged cutting the wires off the detonators ... He cut the wire too short off one of the detonators. It struck fire in his hand and he dropped it on to the floor ... then I saw a blue flame sweeping across the house. The next thing I heard was Captain John Timmins shouting, "Run men, we will all be killed." Almost immediately a terrific explosion occurred.'

The men were preparing detonators and explosives, including gelignite and tonite, for an attack on the RIC barracks in Foulksmills and New Ross. The officer in charge of the IRA unit was John Timmins from Marshalstown, Enniscorthy, who later explained that the blast occurred when flames came into contact with fumes from the explosives.

The five who were killed were from St. Kearns, Saltmills, St. Leonards and Duncormick. The nine survivors were all injured but three escaped arrest. All six who were detained were sent to Portland and later Dartmoor prisons in England. They were released in February 1922 and when they finally returned home, a large crowd that met them at Ballycullane train station escorted the men to their homes by torchlight procession.

Nazi concentration camp's slave labourers from Wexford

Farge concentration camp prisoners at work on the Valentin bunker near Bremen. (photo: Bundesarchiv). Patrick Breen (right) from Wexford was the first Irish prisoner to die in Farge in 1943.

PATRICK BREEN was born in Wexford town on 12 March 1888 to Moses, a baker, and Anne (née Doyle). The family lived on King Street and later in The Faythe, and Patrick worked as an able seaman on merchant ships out of Liverpool.

During World War II, he was on board the Athel Line's MV *Athelfoam* on a voyage from Liverpool to Pastelillo in Cuba. On 15 March 1941, the tanker was attacked by the German Kriegsmarine battleship *Scharnhorst* and sunk by gunfire about 500 miles southeast of Newfoundland. Forty-five survivors, including Patrick, were taken on board as prisoners of war. The next day, the *Scharnhorst* attacked and sank another British merchant freighter, the *Silver Fir*, which was en route to New York. An Irish seaman on board named James Hughes was hit in the neck by shrapnel and died later on the *Scharnhorst*, which had taken all the survivors on board. Two were young Irishmen, Owen Corr from Rush, Co. Dublin and William Kelly from Waterford.

The *Scharnhorst* carried out many sorties into the Atlantic, attacking British merchant shipping during much of the early portion of the war. In 1943, it and several destroyers sortied from Norway and attacked Allied convoys en route to the Soviet Union. During the Battle of the North Cape on 26 December 1943, the Royal Navy battleship HMS *Duke of York* and its escorts sank the *Scharnhorst*. Out of a crew of 1,968 only 36 were rescued.

Just hours after Britain and France declared war on Germany on 3 September 1939, the first casualty was the British transatlantic liner SS *Athenia*. Bound for Montreal on a voyage from Glasgow, via Liverpool and Belfast, the *Athenia* was torpedoed and sunk by German submarine *U-30* about 200 nautical miles northwest of Donegal. Of the more than 1,400 passengers and crew on board, including some 500 Jewish refugees, 117 lives were lost. Many of the survivors, who included Captain James Cook, were landed at Galway and transported to Dublin, from where they returned to Glasgow. News of the unprotected passenger ship's sinking caused a sensation at the time, with Germany denying it had been responsible. But at the Nuremberg trials that followed WWII, the German admiral Karl Dönitz (who succeeded Hitler for just one week following his suicide in 1945), finally admitted that the *Athenia* had been torpedoed by *U-30* and that every effort had been made to cover it up.

The second half of the war saw the tide beginning to turn, with Germany losing control of the skies and defeats on the ground on the Eastern Front and in North Africa. The Allies were gaining the upper hand at sea too. In May 1941, following the capture of the German submarine *U-110* by the Royal Navy and the seizing of its Enigma machine and code books, the Kriegsmarine Enigma code was finally cracked by Britain's code-breaking organization located in Bletchley Park.

Germany responded by developing a revolutionary larger and faster diesel-electric submarine called the *XXI* or *Elektroboot*. It was designed to operate entirely submerged up to several days. But these new U-boats had to be built quickly.

Forced labour and slavery in Nazi Germany reached a peak of about 15 million men and women from twenty European countries during the Second

World War. About two-thirds came from Central and Eastern Europe. There was a particular dependence on these workers for the armaments factories and on construction sites. Many died as a result of their squalid living conditions, malnutrition, mistreatment and torture, as well as from Allied bombing of their workplaces. When Nazi Germany was finally defeated in 1945, approximately 11 million foreigners were freed, most of whom were forced labourers, with many drawn from prisoner-of-war camps.

Patrick Breen and the other 44 survivors of the *Athelfoam* along with the other merchant seamen, who were now prisoners of war, were landed at Brest in German-occupied Brittany by the battleship *Scharnhorst*. From there they were first transported to Drancy internment camp in Paris and later to Milag Nord POW camp, about 19 miles north-east of Bremen. Milag held up to 4,200 internees, mainly captured British merchant seamen. Conditions at the camp were spartan but better than the forced labour and concentration camps across Germany. Several inmates constructed tunnels in attempts to escape but all were re-captured and returned to camp.

Many Irish merchant seamen ended up in Milag. Some were pressured by the Gestapo to collaborate with the Nazi regime by joining German forces or to return to Ireland and spy for them. They suggested to them that, being Irish, they ought to work against Britain in the war but they all refused. They also refused to sign contractual agreements to become voluntary workers for the Third Reich. Offers were made to work in the Messerschmitt aircraft plant or to be employed on the merchant ships out of Hamburg but the Irish prisoners were sceptical and refused all offers. They were told that the alternative was that they were to be sent to labour camps.

CONCENTRATION CAMP

On 6 February 1943, thirty-two Irish prisoners were awoken in the middle of the night by the Gestapo and taken on two lorries to Bremen-Farge. The Neuengamme concentration camp in Hamburg was established in 1938 and by 1943 had 83 sub-camps in northern Germany. Bremen-Farge was the largest, located in Farge, a small inland port on the River Weser near the north German city of Bremen. The camp had been erected close to a naval fuel oil storage facility and some of the prisoners were held in an empty underground fuel tank until the new slave-labour concentration camp was completed.

Initially the camp was run by the SS. The prisoners at Farge were used as slave labour to construct the massive bomb-proof Valentin submarine construction facility, the largest in Germany, between 1943 and 1945. It was planned to begin assembly of the *XXI* submarine there, starting in April 1945.

Up to 12,000 slave workers from seven concentration camps were used to build the gigantic Valentin bunker. These were mainly non-German inmates and included Russian, Polish and French prisoners of war as well as the Irish merchant seamen. It is estimated that by the end of the war 6,000 workers had died in the construction of the submarine factory — more than half of the workforce.

Conditions at Bremen-Farge were horrendous. About an hour after the Irishmen arrived the beatings by a group of SS guards with weighted hosepipes began. The prisoners' heads were shaved, they were deloused and all personal possessions confiscated. The Irish seamen were told by the SS that they were no longer being held under the protection of the Geneva Convention and they would have no further contact with the outside world.

The largest German slave-labour and extermination camp, Auschwitz in the Polish town of Oświęcim, which was annexed by Nazi Germany in 1939. Above the entrance it reads 'Work Sets You Free', photographed in the 1970s. (photo: Des Kiely)

For two years they lived in hellish conditions. Many prisoners died of disease, starvation and exhaustion in the camp or on the construction site. Others were beaten to death or shot on the spot.

At first the Irish prisoners were put to work laying the railway tracks leading to the planned Valentin bunker that were necessary before construction began. They worked alongside young Jewish women aged 16 to 18 from Eastern Europe, who had also been taken to the Farge camp. They worked in all weather, often in below-freezing temperatures in flimsy clothing. Prisoners caught wearing sacks, extra fabric or pieces of blankets under their shirts were beaten or shot. Instead of socks, they wrapped rags around their feet.

Work on the Valentin assembly plant site continued day and night, with the prisoners working at least 12-hour shifts and Admiral Dönitz reporting directly to Hitler on its progress. Foundations were laid more than 50 feet deep and when completed the roof of the bunker was almost 25 feet thick in order to withstand bombing. Each section of the giant electric submarine was to be built throughout Germany and transported to the new facility. A door on its western wall would open into the River Weser to allow completed submarines to enter the river directly and on into the North Sea. It was designed to build the most modern and deadly submarines in the German fleet at a rate of one every 56 hours.

Each day at the Farge camp started with a roll call that could take one hour while the prisoners were forced to stand to attention without speaking. They were beaten and then marched the three or four miles to the Valentin site, which they reached around 6am, and had to start work immediately. Those who were put to work moving huge steel and iron girders often perished in accidents. These detachments were known as 'suicide squads'. Many workers collapsed and died from exhaustion, some run over by trucks. At the end of each day they were marched back to Farge, where they had to wait for up to two hours in silence before finally getting a bowl of watery turnip soup. Many died from starvation. The Irish in Farge were the only group whose first language was English and they tried to stick together in the hope that they might survive the appalling conditions.

But on 13 May 1943, only three months after arriving at Bremen-Farge, Patrick Breen from Wexford town died aged 55. He was the first of five Irish merchant seamen to lose his life in the camp. His death was recorded as being as a result of pneumonia but one account said he died from a beating with an iron bar by one of the camp guards. It is not known what happened to his body but in all probability he was buried in one of the mass graves close to the camp.

Typhus often broke out in Nazi concentration camps. Spread by lice, mites and fleas and highly contagious, the guards often responded by executing those infected. In 1941, the Neuengamme camp in Hamburg was hit with an outbreak of typhus which was left untreated and at least 1,000 Soviet prisoners were left to die.

William Knott from Ringsend,
Dublin survived Farge.

Gerald O'Hara from Ballina,
Co. Mayo died in Farge in 1944.

William Knox from Dublin was
the last Irishman to die in Farge.

Typhus hit Farge in 1944 and caused the deaths of three of the Irish inmates. Gerald O'Hara (50) a radio officer from Ballina, Co. Mayo died on 15 March 1944. A month later, Owen Corr (23) from Rush, Co. Dublin and Thomas Murphy (53), also from Dublin, both died on the same day: 27 April 1944.

William Warnock was replaced as Irish chargé d'affaires in Berlin by Con Cremin in 1944. One of the merchant seamen held in Milag Nord POW camp was Christopher Ryan from Tramore, Co. Waterford. He too was transferred with the other Irish prisoners to Farge concentration camp. A letter addressed to the Swiss consul in Bremen, pleading for help and signed by the remaining Irish inmates, was secretly taken out of the camp by a Swiss national who was being released. The letter made its way to Cremin in Berlin and he soon arrived at the camp, escorted by SS officers, to meet the men. He stayed for about two hours and was shocked at their physical condition, and promised that he would have them repatriated to Ireland.

Late in 1944, the Irishmen were put on a train to the port of Flensburg on the Danish border. The plan was that they were to be taken to Ireland on board a Swedish merchant ship. But Allied planes had destroyed a bridge on the route to Flensburg and the ship that was to have taken them to Sweden had left without them. The men were returned to Farge and not to Milag, despite protests from Cremin.

The fifth and last Irishman to die in the camp was William Knox from Dún Laoghaire, Co. Dublin. Knox (59) was the oldest of the remaining Irish prisoners. It is believed that he may have died from oedema, also known as fluid retention. The village doctor was called and he was operated on without anaesthetic while four of his Irish colleagues held him down on a table. The doctor inserted a tube into his side and drained some water from him. But he died two days later on 2 March 1945, just two months before Germany signed an unconditional surrender on 8 May 1945, marking the end of the Second World War.

On 27 March 1945, the Valentin site was attacked by a squadron of twenty RAF bombers but the roof was only partially damaged in two places. Work on the bunker continued until 9 April and Bremen was in Allied hands by the end of the month.

In 1944, 5,000 slave workers in the Neuengamme camp complex died with 6,000 more in the first three months of 1945. With the Allies already close to Bremen by March 1945, the SS began to evacuate the remaining estimated 20,000 inmates in Farge and the other satellite camps and vast quantities of files were burned. The SS camp Kommandant at Bremen-Farge was Heinrich Schauwecker. With the defeat of the Nazis now imminent, he shot sixteen prisoners after announcing that he knew he would be either shot or hanged by the Allies and said: "I will take as many as I can with me." The SS executed another 58 men and 18 women before leaving. The prisoners were moved farther from the Allied lines to other camps such as Bergen-Belsen, where many thousands starved to death and around 8,000 Jewish prisoners were slaughtered. A thousand inmates, some from Neuengamme, were burned to death in an orgy of killing, helped by some of the local population, in a barn outside the town of Gardelegen. Two days later, the charred remains were found by advancing U.S. troops, who forced over 200 local men to recover the bodies and bury them in individual graves.

The Irish inmates had been moved back to Milag Nord POW camp, where the other prisoners were shocked at their condition. They had not seen them for two years and had believed that they had volunteered to work for the Germans. The camp was liberated by British troops on 27 April 1945. Within a few days the Irish survivors were flown to England and some were soon on a ship on their way home to Ireland. Many were weak, malnourished and seriously ill and would not recover for several years.

Survivor James Furlong from The Faythe had moved to England in 1916 to complete his apprenticeship as a marine engineer with Cammell Laird shipbuilders in Birkenhead. He joined the merchant navy the following year and remained living in England. In 1940, while on board the SS *Duquesa* out of Liverpool, the vessel was captured in the South Atlantic by the German battleship *Admiral Scheer*. Now suffering from rheumatism, James wrote to the British Foreign Office in 1966 requesting compensation and was awarded £1,000. He thanked them but asked for more and received a further £1,385 and wrote back: "I am a very happy man now as I have paid off the mortgage on my house and have a few pounds left over which will come in handy." He wrote that he spent his time in Farge "always afraid my turn would come".

Another Wexfordman who survived the horror and returned to Ireland was Thomas Cooney from Monck Street. It is believed that he had first been intercepted on a neutral Liberty ship (they were mass-produced in the U.S. for wartime use), released and transferred to a Swedish ship, only to be captured again by the German navy.

The death in Farge of Patrick Breen from Wexford town was not reported back home until the end of the war when William English from Arklow, one of the 32 Irish prisoners, spoke to the *Irish Times* in May 1945. On 17 May, the newspaper mistakenly reported that Patrick hailed from Blackwater and this was repeated in other publications. *The Free Press* went in search of his family in Blackwater and reported on 26 May that "Exhaustive inquiries made by *The Free Press* failed to trace his relatives in Blackwater." Most of the Irish survivors never spoke of their time incarcerated in Nazi Germany and their fate has been

Part of the monstrous Valentin U-boat assembly plant, by far the largest in Germany, is now a tourist attraction.

largely ignored. The surviving Irishmen were awarded between £1,000 and £2,400 each by the British government.

In 1946, trials took place for the war crimes committed in the Neuengamme camp network. Seven SS members were consequently hanged. Four of the surviving Irish seamen travelled to Hamburg in the following year to attend a British military court. Twelve of the Farge guards were on trial and five of them were charged with multiple murders. In 1999, the German government set up the Forced Labour Compensation Fund. Volkswagen was one of the main contributors, having been compelled to admit in court the previous year that 80 per cent of their workforce during the Second World War had consisted of slave labourers. The Volkswagen car had been the brainchild of Ferdinand Porsche and Adolf Hitler. Porsche was a friend of both Hitler and his second-in-command, Heinrich Himmler. However, it was not until 2004 that the few Irish survivors of Bremen-Farge still living received any payment from the fund.

The memorial sculpture at the Valentin bunker, unveiled in 1983 and called 'Annihilation Through Work', was created by Bremen artist Fritz Stein.

At the end of the war the Valentin bunker was still unfinished and not a single *XXI* submarine had been built at the complex. With a floor area the size of six football pitches, the bunker was used by the German Army as a storage depot until it was offered for sale in 2010 as a commercial warehouse, but it failed to sell. Part of the structure has now been turned into 'a monument to the cruelty and fiendish technological capabilities of Nazi Germany.' Patrick Breen's name appears on the Tower Hill Memorial in London that commemorates the more than 35,800 merchant seamen who have no known grave.

Southeast's largest freshwater lake – created in the 1850s

The man-made Lower Lake, looking towards Johnstown Castle and visitor centre. (photo courtesy Irish Heritage Trust)

THE LOWER LAKE at Johnstown Castle is the largest freshwater lake in County Wexford and surrounding counties, covering some 14 acres. Tacumshin Lake and Lady's Island Lake, though much bigger, are both brackish, i.e. they have a mix of fresh water and salt water. The artificial Lower Lake was created in the 1850s as part of the complete restyling of Johnstown Castle and landscaping of the estate.

The present castle was constructed around the original three-storey tower house built by the English knight Geoffrey de Esmonde, who arrived from Lincolnshire in 1171 in the wake of the Anglo-Norman invasion of 1169. The Catholic Esmondes also built Rathlannon tower house, which still stands on the grounds of Johnstown demesne. William Esmonde of

Johnstown and Marcus Esmonde of Rathlannon had their estates confiscated by Cromwellian forces in 1649. Johnstown was granted to Lt. Col. Overstreet, a Cromwellian soldier. The estate soon passed to John Reynolds, a Wexford merchant, whose eldest daughter Mary married John Grogan in 1682. The Grogans resided in Johnstown tower house and added a second tower next to the original. A descendant, another John Grogan, married his cousin Catherine Knox, heiress of nearby Rathmacknee Castle. Their son Thomas was killed while serving with the Castletown Yeomanry Cavalry (Gorey) in the Battle of Arklow on 9 June 1798. Their eldest, Cornelius, MP for Enniscorthy from 1769 to 1773 and High Sheriff of Wexford for 1779, was in possession of Johnstown Castle at the time. He was court-martialled for complicity in the insurrection and hanged on Wexford Bridge on 28 June 1798.

The Johnstown estate was seized by the Crown following the Rebellion. Twelve years later, on payment of the heavy penalty of £10,000, it was restored in 1810 to John Grogan, another brother of Cornelius, who embarked on its remodelling, using the services of the English architect James Pain. His son Hamilton was born in 1807 to his second wife Elizabeth FitzGerald. John died in 1815 when Hamilton was still a young boy. In 1829, he married his first cousin Sophia Rowe, a niece of Cornelius Grogan. Hamilton and Sophia continued the work of reconstructing Johnstown Castle. Hamilton inherited other lands on the death of his relative Samuel Morgan and so became the largest untitled landowner in Ireland with other estates in counties Wexford, Wicklow, West-

Hamilton Grogan, his wife Sophia and 3-year-old daughter Elizabeth. (Painted in 1833 by the London artist Edmund Parris, who was later commissioned to produce a series of paintings of the castle in 1847).

meath and Offaly. He was the second-largest landowner in County Wexford, with over 15,000 acres.

Hamilton employed the services of the architect Daniel Robertson, who was largely associated with the Gothic Revival style of the 1830s. Robertson also designed Castleboro House, Wells House, Wilton Castle and Ballinkeele House and was a noted landscape designer, having been responsible for the gardens at Powerscourt House and Killruddery House in County Wicklow.

Daniel Robertson (c.1770-1849), architect and landscape designer.

Robertson was born in the USA to a Scottish father and was married to Irish-born Amelia Clarke. He was twice declared bankrupt in England and was even imprisoned for debt. He moved to Ireland in the early 1830s, where he received a series of commissions, which included designing the terraces in the Italian garden at Powerscourt. However, according to Lord Powerscourt, he was crippled with severe gout and advanced alcoholism and was 'always in debt and…used to hide in the domes of the roof of the house' to escape the Sheriff's officers who pursued him. He 'used to be wheeled out on the terrace in a wheelbarrow with a bottle of sherry, and as long as that lasted he was able to design and direct the workmen, but when the sherry was finished he collapsed and was incapable of working till the drunken fit had evaporated.' He died aged about 79 in Howth, County Dublin in 1849.

Robertson had a great interest in medieval castle architecture which was popular in Victorian times. Between 1835 and 1849, together with the Wexford architect Martin Day from Kilmore, he worked with Hamilton Grogan to create the neo-medieval embattled castle, fortified gate lodges and romantic gardens. A model of Johnstown Castle was exhibited at the Great Exhibition of 1851 held in Hyde Park, London.

They had the five-acre Castle Lake dug out and added a folly turret, known as the 'fishing tower', a square tower and a terrace with a row of statues positioned on the far side of the lake, directly opposite the castle.

The Lower Lake covers some fourteen acres and was created in the 1850s by building a dam at the southern end of this valley and allowing the overflow

The Castle Lake was created in the 1830s and was the first of the three lakes to be excavated manually.
(photo courtesy Ireland from the Skies)

from the Castle Lake to gradually form the new lake.

When Hamilton Grogan died aged 46 in 1854 his widow Sophia married Sir Thomas Esmonde of Ballynastragh House, near Gorey, two years later. Esmonde, who came to live in the castle, was a descendant of the original owners. The couple retained Martin Day and continued with renovation work on the property.

The demesne subsequently passed to Hamilton Grogan's daughter Jane *(see page 91)*, who married George Forbes of Castle Forbes, Longford, in 1858. The estate finally passed to their second daughter Adelaide (*b.*1860), who married Maurice FitzGerald, son of Charles FitzGerald, the Duke of Leinster, of Carton House, Co. Kildare in 1880.

It was during the time of the FitzGeralds that the smallest and highest of the three lakes, the Garden Lake, to the west of the castle, was dug out in the 1880s. This two-acre lake is fed off the Kildavin stream about a mile away and in turn the lake feeds into the Castle Lake via a stream running close to Rathlannon tower house. Duck decoys were used here for waterfowl hunting. North of the Garden Lake are the four-acre walled gardens built in the 1840s and designed by Daniel Robertson. The upper section, which is closed to the public, contains the head gardener's house where he and his family resided and was later home to the chief steward. James Pierce of Pierce's Foundry designed an under-floor heating system for the glasshouses that once stood here and where exotic fruits were grown. The first banana ever cultivated in County Wexford was grown here.

All three lakes provide homes for a wide range of waterfowl: mute swans, mallards, moorhens and coots. Herons and otters are also found in the Lower Lake. Over 20 peafowl can be found in the gardens as well as red squirrels and pine martens.

Close to the Garden Lake is the FitzGerald family cemetery where Maurice, who died in 1901, Adelaide and their two daughters are buried. Their son Gerald was killed in action in WWI. When Adelaide died in 1942, the estate was gifted to the State by her grandson, Maurice Lakin. The one remaining

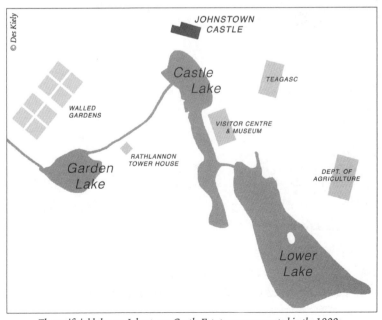

The artificial lakes on Johnstown Castle Estate were excavated in the 1800s.

tower house was deemed unsafe and was later demolished. The main timber staircase suffered from dry rot and was replaced by two stone staircases.

The overflow channel from the Castle Lake was created in the 1850s to create the Lower Lake, the largest on the estate.

Between 1946 and 1958, Johnstown Castle served as a residential horticultural college and agricultural research facility. The farm buildings house the Irish Agricultural Museum, which opened in 1979 and has extensive exhibits of farming and rural life in Ireland. Teagasc, the Agriculture and Food Development Authority, occupy over half of the 1,000-acre Johnstown demesne. They run dairy and bull beef research farms on the estate and the country's leading state-of-the-art research centre for soils, air and water quality and the agricultural environment. The new Johnstown Castle visitor centre opened in 2019 and the estate is now run by the Irish Heritage Trust, an independent charity, for Teagasc. Guided tours of the castle are offered to the public and they include a walk through the 86-metre servants' tunnel – considered to be Ireland's longest domestic tunnel.

The smallest of the three lakes, the Garden Lake or upper lake, was dug out in the 1880s during the occupation by the FitzGerald family. (photo: Des Kiely)

Ardcandrisk House: haunted by ghost of Lady Dane's cousin

Ardcandrisk House c.1900. The house was deemed haunted about twenty years later, abandoned by its new owner and left to fall into ruin. (photo: Robert French/National Library of Ireland)

ARDCANDRISK (*Ard Caoinrois* in Irish, meaning high ground above a forested promontory), is a townland bounded on the north by the River Slaney and on the road from Ferrycarrig to Killurin. The railway from Wexford to Enniscorthy traverses the pretty wooded countryside, where Ardcandrisk House was constructed in 1833 on an 84-acre estate.

When Samuel Morgan, twice Mayor of Waterford (1779 and 1801), died in 1827 his estates were shared equally by Hamilton Grogan of Johnstown and his brother George of Ardcandrisk. Both added the name Morgan to their own by royal licence the following year. Hamilton was responsible for the construction of the Johnstown Castle that we see today.

Hamilton's eldest daughter, Elizabeth *(see painting of her as a child on page 84)*, married Robert Deane, son of the 3rd Baron Muskerry, of Springfield Castle in County Limerick in 1847. Elizabeth and Robert took up residence in Ardcandrisk House. On the death of Hamilton in 1854, they similarly assumed the additional name Morgan. Elizabeth and Robert Deane-Morgan together owned vast estates in counties Cork, Limerick, Clare, Tipperary,

Kilkenny, Waterford and Wexford.

The kitchen quarters were located in the basement of the house. In the kitchen-yard were the dairy, laundry and female living apartments; the bachelor employees lived in the stable-yard, accessible through a tunnel leading from the house. The farmyard and cowsheds were to the rear of the stables and separated from them by a belfry arch. The bell was rung three times daily: 6am to start the day, 12 noon for dinner and 6pm to cease work. Nearly every family in the Barntown area depended on the estate for work. Ten house servants were employed, six men worked in the stable and farmyard and twelve in the gardens. The head steward and head gardener and their families lived in two fine two-storied houses situated near the orchard, and are still occupied today.

Florence Gonne-Bell, who moved into Ardcandrisk with her cousin Lady Dane (seated), on the death of her husband. (Photo source: The Mary Hughes Collection)

Elizabeth and Robert Deane-Morgan's only son was born in 1854, the same year that her father Hamilton Grogan died, and so they named him Hamilton. Robert passed away just four years later aged 46 and Elizabeth inherited the Ardcandrisk estate. She continued to reside there and invited her young cousin Florence Gonne-Bell to move from Streamstown, County Mayo to join her as a lady companion and also to help with the management of the household. Her son Hamilton was aged only 14 when his grandfather, the 3rd Baron Muskerry, died in 1868. He inherited the Springfield Castle demesne in County Limerick and succeeded as the 4th Baron Muskerry.

The widow Elizabeth Deane-Morgan, known locally as 'Lady Dane', was considered a good landlady who treated her employees well. At Christmas time each worker was given a stone of beef, a pound of tea and a stone of sugar and the resident seamstress made a red petticoat for each of the female ser-vants. All the employees and their families were invited to a Christmas party in the billiard-room at the house.

Lady Dane had the gardens carefully tended and the lawns manicured. There was a terraced garden at the front of the house and she would accompany visitors on a stroll through the many scenic walks lined with rhododendrons and exotic flowers. The walled orchard and vegetable garden provided the produce necessary for the house and kitchen and the grounds had three tennis courts, said to be the finest in County Wexford. One path led to a bridge over the railway track to the Slaney, from where she would often sail to St. Iberius Church in Wexford to attend religious services.

Rarely seen without her two Irish wolfhounds, Rae and Lou, and her small Pekingese dogs by her side, Lady Dane was a renowned animal lover and excellent horse-rider. She was a patroness of the County Wexford Society for the Prevention of Cruelty to Animals and had drinking troughs positioned along the roads in the area. One can be still be seen close to the railway bridge at Ferrycarrig. In 1888, she had the famous swan water trough installed in The Faythe area of Wexford town on behalf of the society.

There was a traditional belief that on the death of their father Hamilton, Elizabeth and her sister Jane, having been jointly left Johnstown Castle estate, agreed to settle the ownership on the result of a horse-race from Ardcandrisk. The first through the gates of the castle would become the new owner. Elizabeth, concerned for her animal's welfare, stopped on the way to water her horse, while her sister continued on to Johnstown. Jane was first to arrive at the gates and duly claimed her prize of the castle and estate.

Lady Dane of Ardcandrisk House was an animal lover and patroness of County Wexford Society for the Prevention of Cruelty to Animals. In 1888, she had the iconic swan drinking trough installed in The Faythe in Wexford town. (photo: Robert French/National Library of Ireland)

The Primrose League, founded in England in 1883, was an organization set up to spread the politics of the Tory Party. Lady Dane was one of the founder members of the Wexford branch and the first meeting was held in Ardcandrisk House in 1886. Named the Wexford Habitation, and with Susie Elgee appointed honorary secretary and treasurer, the League was a society of the local ascendancy. Reporting on a meeting held at Ardcandrisk in 1895, the *Primrose League Gazette* concluded its report saying: '*The weather was very fine and a most enjoyable afternoon was spent. A vote of thanks was passed to Mrs Deane Morgan for her kindness in giving Ardcandrisk for the meeting, and the National Anthem having been sung, the meeting then dispersed.*'

Lady Dane reached 70 with the turn of the century and her health was deteriorating. Eventually confined to her residence and in a wheelchair, two servants pushed her around the house and gardens. A lift, operated by a winch from the attic, provided her with access to the bedroom floor. In May 1920, she caught a cold that developed into bronchitis and died at Ardcandrisk, aged 91. Her obituary notice in *The Free Press* referred to her as ... '*a generous contributor towards all projects for charitable purposes ... in the management of Wexford County Infirmary, of which she was a life governor, she took a deep interest and frequently sent donations to assist in the alleviation of the lot of its inmates.*' Lady Dane was interred in the family vault at Rathaspeck.

She bequeathed Ardcandrisk to her cousin Florence Gonne-Bell, who had been her companion for over sixty years. But Florence herself died just nine months later in February 1921, aged 82. She left the estate to her niece, Mrs. Florence Harvey (née Irvine), who occupied the house for just a few months before disposing of Lady Dane's goods and chattels in a two-day auction in December 1921. After the death of Lady Dane, many local people found themselves unemployed for the first time in their lives.

All that remains of Ardcandrisk House today.
(photo: Michael Brazzill)

CAPTAIN COOKMAN

The next owner of Ardcandrisk estate was Captain Nathaniel Cookman of Monart House, The Still, outside Enniscorthy. His father was Edward Cookman who had married Sarah Davis of Fairfield. His grandfather married for a second time in 1859, when he wed Isabella Jameson of Daphne Castle. She was a daughter of Andrew Jameson, who set up the Fairfield whiskey distillery in 1818. Andrew's father and brother established John Jameson & Son eight years earlier in Dublin. Isabella's sister Annie married Giuseppe Marconi, an Italian aristocrat, and their son was the inventor Guglielmo.

Cookman was educated in Kent and served in the First World War. He saw action in Flanders as a lieutenant in the Royal Field Artillery, later gaining the rank of captain. He was awarded the Queen's Meritorious' Award for acts of gallantry many years later. He married Dorothy Davis, a cousin of Marconi, in 1921 and they had four children: Nathaniel, Edlyne, Elydyr and Dorothy.

On acquiring Ardcandrisk, his family lived in the house while the land was rented out to a Patrick Broaders. Cookman had a flair for electricals and gadgetry and had the first electricity generator in the area installed. Everything was going fine for the Cookmans in Ardcandrisk House until one night, according to local belief, Nathaniel witnessed a ghostly apparition on the stairs. His dog became very agitated and attacked its master. He later claimed it was the ghost of Florence Gonne-Bell. From that night on, Captain Cookman refused to spend another night in the house and instead slept on his boat that was moored on the Slaney. This signalled the beginning of the end of Ardcandrisk House. Nathaniel sold every item of value in numerous auctions and Patrick Broaders purchased the estate, which is now farmed by his grandson. The house fell into ruin and is today an empty shell.

Captain Cookman ended his days back in Monart House, where he died in 1983. His daughter Dorothy Oakes sold Monart to the Griffin Hotel Group in 2002 and it now operates as the five-star Monart Spa Hotel.

The grounds of Ardcandrisk House were the location of the infamous duel between rival politicians John Colclough of Tintern Abbey and William Alcock of Wilton Castle on that fateful day of 30 May 1807, when Colclough was shot dead. (*See Fascinating Wexford History, Volume One*).

Grateful thanks to Tom and Teresa Wickham for their research included in this story.

The Norse Vikings who founded the town of Veisafjǫrðr

'Havhingsten fra Glendalough' (Sea Stallion from Glendalough), a reconstruction of the original Viking longship built circa 1042 near Dublin with oak from Glendalough, County Wicklow. This replica was built in Roskilde, Denmark between 2000 and 2004. Approximately 30m long, it was one of the longest Viking ships ever found. In 2007 the replica ship sailed from Roskilde to Dublin on a research trip taking six weeks to complete.

SEA WARRIORS from Norway, Denmark and Sweden, who carried out raids on many parts of Europe and North Africa from the 8th century for over 300 years, were known as Vikings, though they called themselves *Ostmen* (Eastmen). They plundered many settlements on the coasts of Western Europe, from Scotland to Sicily. The Vikings also sailed across the North Atlantic and conquered the Faroe Islands, Iceland and Greenland. They reached Newfoundland 500 years before Christopher Columbus discovered North America. They also travelled east as far as Constantinople and the Caspian Sea and established the Rus dynasty, from which Russia and Belarus are believed to have derived their names.

The Viking shallow-draught longships were wide, long and light and designed for speed. They could navigate waters only one-metre deep and were capable of making beach landings. Almost the entire length was fitted with shields and oars. The bow and stern were symmetrical, allowing for quick change of direction without turning.

Ireland at the time of the arrival of the Vikings was a Gaelic, rural society divided into kingdoms and over the past 400 years had become almost entirely Christian. Monastic towns played an important role in religious, political, economic and cultural life. The old south Leinster lordship of Uí Ceinnsealaig (Kinsella) was founded in the 5th century. Centred in Ferns, their kingdom covered an area a little larger than the current County Wexford and included parts of Wicklow and Carlow. Cairpre Mac Cathail was king of Uí Ceinnsealaig around the time of the first Viking raid on the Celtic settlement of Loch gCarman – named after Carmán, the mythological Greek female warrior and sorceress who was supposedly buried in the area. It took place in the year AD 819 on the monastery on Begerin Island in the shallow northern area of Wexford harbour. These pagan Scandinavians had already plundered the monastery on the island of Lindisfarne, off the northeast coast of England, in 793 – traditionally considered the start of the Viking age. Two years later, they carried out their first recorded attack in Ireland when they raided Lambay Island. St. Columba is said to have established a monastic settlement on the island in about AD 530. Lambay's church and its buildings were burned in the attack in 795. This was followed by a further assault on the coast north of Dublin in 798 and on the Connacht coast in 807.

Monasteries that could be reached by ship were irresistible targets, where valuables as well as food were to be found. St. Ibar or Iberius, patron saint of Wexford, founded a church, monastery and school on Begerin Island in the shallow waters of the northern area of Loch gCarman in the year 420. Ibar instructed his pupils in sacred literature on the island up to his death, recorded as 23 April 500. During reclamation work in 1847-49 to create the North Slobs, it was discovered that the island had been connected to Dairinis Island to the south by a narrow bridge or causeway. Two rows of oak piles, about four feet apart and in a straight line, were found when the land was drained. It is speculated that Begerin was also connected to the mainland.

It is recorded that Ferns too was plundered in 835 and later burned in a further attack four years later. The Vikings established a *longphort* or fortress for their longships at Wexford harbour, possibly around the deep pool, now incorporated in the present-day Crescent Quay. By 888 they had founded a new settlement – initially separate to Loch gCarman. They gave the estuary of the Slaney the name Veisafjǫrðr, said to mean 'inlet of mud flats' in Old Norse. The communities of Loch gCarman and Veisafjǫrðr eventually merged into one town known later as Waesfjord, then Wexford.

The Vikings established other *longphorts* along the Irish coast from where raiding parties were carried out inland by sailing up rivers and then retreating back to their coastal bases. They plundered churches and monastic sites such as Clonmacnoise, Glendalough and Lismore. The settlements of Dyflin (Dublin), Veðrafjǫrðr (Waterford), Cork and Limerick were attacked and through intermarriage with the native Irish, this eventually resulted in the emergence of the Hiberno-Norse people.

The Scandinavian invaders accepted Christianity over the course of the next 200 years and built churches in their towns. In Wexford, the parishes of St. Mary's, St. Patrick's, St. Iberius and St. Doologhue's (Olaf's) are believed to have stood within the precinct of the old Norse town. Stonebridge, located near the bottom of South Main Street, crossed the Bishopswater stream, which may have been close to the southern boundary of the Norse settlement.

Keysers Lane runs east and west off South Main Street. *Keysers* meant 'quays' in Old Norse and in modern Norwegian the word is *kaiers*. The lane separated the parishes of St. Patrick and St. Iberius and ran all the way from present-day School Street to Crescent Quay. Similar street names are found in the Viking cities of Dublin, Cork and Waterford. There was a Keysers Lane located close to St. Audoen's Church in the heart of medieval Dublin that ran down to the Liffey quays. Keysers Hill in Cork connects with the River Lee, and Keysers Street in Waterford links High Street and the quays.

To date there is little arch-aeological evidence of Viking defences in Wexford, in part because their early constructions would have been of timber. One of the few literary references to Viking walls is found in *Expugnatio Hibernica (Conquest of Ireland)*, written by the medieval historian Giraldus Cambrensis (Gerald of Wales) in 1189, twenty years after the Anglo-Norman invasion

The original Keysers ('quays') Lane off South Main Street dates back to the old Norse settlement when it ran down as far as the waterfront at Crescent Quay. (photo: Des Kiely)

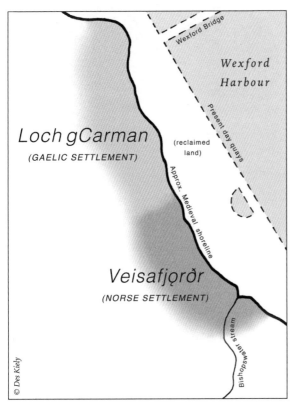

Conjectural map of the old Gaelic and Norse settlements about a thousand years ago, before any land reclamation.

Map labels: Wexford Bridge · Wexford Harbour · Present day quays · Loch gCarman (GAELIC SETTLEMENT) · (reclaimed land) · Approx. Medieval shoreline · Veisafjǫrðr (NORSE SETTLEMENT) · Bishopswater stream · © Des Kiely

of Ireland. He relates the story of the Anglo-Norman attack on the town in 1169 and how the inhabitants "burned the suburbs, forthwith retired within their walls" and the attackers then "posted archers so as to command the advanced towers". In another account he wrote that a Norman soldier was killed by a stone thrown from the wall and after which he fell "headlong into the ditch". This indicates that Wexford had a wall with defensive towers and a ditch when the Anglo-Normans arrived.

In 1987, while carrying out exploratory work on foundations for the construction of a new building (Colman Doyle's) on the corner of Bride Street and South Main Street, timber was discovered protruding from the black muddy ground. An archaeological dig was carried out the following year and artefacts including pieces of leather, pottery, animal bones and shells from the medieval period were uncovered. Evidence of a building sequence between the years 1000 to 1300 was found with the remains of 15 wattle houses. Two of the houses, similar to those found at Wood Quay, Dublin in the 1970s, were described as Viking and from the early 11th century.

The Vikings who settled in Ireland are believed to have come from Norway, a country that had no towns. They were country people who were engaged in farming, fishing and hunting but were expert shipbuilders. Loch gCarman together with Veisafjǫrðr evolved as a town over the next 200 years or so before the arrival of the Anglo-Normans. Both the Irish and Old Norse languages (with similarities to present-day Icelandic and Faroese) were spoken during this time, known as the Viking age or Hiberno-Norse period. Many

Old Norse placenames survive, such as Selskar (*seal rock*) and Tuskar (*large rock*) — *skar* meaning rock, Saltee (*salt island*), *ee* meaning island and Carnsore (a combination of the Irish word *carn*, meaning pile, and the Old Norse word *eyrr*, meaning headland).

Hiberno-Norse silver penny, minted in Dyflin (Dublin), AD 1002-1008.

The Vikings also settled areas of the hinterland for farming in order to provide the town with produce and raw material. They minted the first coins in Ireland from about 996 in Dublin, in the reign of Sigtrygg Olafsson (Sitric), the Hiberno-Norse king of Dublin. The silver coins followed the designs of those minted in other Viking colonies abroad and were used mainly for trading with them.

The Duchy of Normandy was created by the Vikings on the north coast of France in 911 and its first ruler was the Nordmann, or Norwegian, Rollo. In 1066, his descendant William of Normandy conquered England and was crowned the first Norman King of England. A century later the Anglo-Normans turned their attention to Ireland.

The Irish National Heritage Park in Ferrycarrig tells the history of human habitation in Ireland up to the Anglo-Norman invasion at Bannow in 1169. Set in forty acres of natural wooded marshland, a replica Viking harbour has been recreated on the banks of the Slaney complete with a Viking house, based on the house remains found during the Bride Street excavations in 1988.

The Oseberg longship was discovered at Tønsberg in southern Norway, regarded as the oldest city in Norway, founded by Vikings in the 9th century. The ship was located under a burial mound in 1903 and is on display in the Viking Ship Museum at Bygdøy.
(photo: Des Kiely, 1990)

Two 'Whiteboys' hanged for Tomfarney farm murders

A typical eviction scene in rural Ireland with the landlord, helped by bailiffs and members of the RIC, enforcing the removal of tenants either unable or refusing to pay their rent. (photo: National Library of Ireland)

THE REDMONDS were evicted from their farm in the townland of Tomfarney, near Bree, for the non-payment of £5 rent owed to the landlord. This resulted in two members of the new tenant family and a policeman being shot dead in a revenge attack in November 1832. The killers were members of the local Whiteboys or Whitefeet.

The Whiteboys and the Ribbonmen were secret peasant societies formed in the 18th and 19th centuries to oppose evictions, using sabotage and violence against unscrupulous landlords. The violence came to a head during the Tithe War of 1831-36, when Catholics were obliged to pay tithes, or taxes, to the Protestant Church of Ireland. To respond to the upsurge in violence, the Royal Irish Constabulary were deployed to confront civil unrest in rural areas. In Newtownbarry (Bunclody), 14 men were killed by yeomen (the mainly Protestant militia) in 1831 in protests over the payment of tithes (see story in *Fascinating Wexford History, Volume One*). The incident raised tensions even further and unrest escalated across the county.

On 1 March 1833, James Jackman, a Whiteboy, was tried in Wexford Courthouse that then stood on Commercial Quay, opposite the old wooden

Wexford Bridge. He was accused of murdering John Roche in the townland of Old Court, Adamstown. Jackman's father had been evicted from his farm for the non-payment of rent and the holding was then transferred to the Roche family. James Jackman was sentenced to be hanged on 4 March but his sentence was commuted to transportation for life. He was most likely banished to one of the penal colonies in New Holland (known later as Australia).

Jackman's brother, Nicholas, was alleged to have also been a supporter of the local Whiteboys. Another member was 19-year-old John Redmond, the youngest of seven brothers. His family were evicted from their farmhouse in Tomfarney, near Bree. His father had lived there for almost sixty years but when the rent fell into arrears and £5 was owed to the landlord, he was unable to pay. The Redmonds were removed from the property and the house and farm passed to another family, the Maddocks.

There was great resentment in the locality towards the eviction of the Redmonds as well as towards the new tenants, Edmund and Mary Maddock and their four children. Shortly after they moved in, threatening notes were delivered to the house and an attempt was made to burn the property down. This resulted in two policemen being assigned to the farmhouse to protect them. On the night of 22 November 1832, an armed group of Whiteboys torched the house with the family and policemen inside, most of whom were in bed. When the two RIC men opened the front door, they were met with a volley of gunfire. One of them, Joseph Wright from Glynn, was killed instantly but the other managed to escape. As the rest of the household tried to flee the flames, Mary Maddock and her daughter Margaret were shot dead, while one of her sons, despite having received two musket balls in the chest, survived. Edmund Maddock was badly wounded but escaped with two of his children. His youngest son hid in nearby bushes, from where he could observe some of the Whiteboys.

In the aftermath of the atrocity, the youngest Maddock boy was taken into police protection in Wexford barracks. He was able to identify two of the Whiteboys as John Redmond and Nicholas Jackman. The pair were arrested and held in Wexford Jail, then located at the junction of Hill Street and Spawell Road, until their trial about three months later on Saturday, 2 March 1833.

They were tried before Judge John Leslie Foster and a jury in Wexford Courthouse. Foster was Baron of the Court of Exchequer, one of the Four

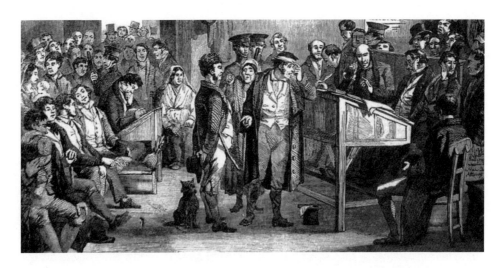

Courts in Dublin. The main witness was Maddock's youngest son, who identified both defendants as the perpetrators of the shooting dead of his mother and sister as well as the policeman. They were both found guilty of the murder of Constable Wright, Mary Maddock and her daughter Margaret. Before passing sentence, the judge instructed them to rise and asked if there was any reason why they should not both face the executioner.

Jackman addressed the court and declared: *"Whatever time I part this life, the Kingdom of Heaven, or the sight of God, may I never see, if I was out of my house for half an hour on the night of the attack on the house of the Maddocks; and if the Jury, or any Lord on this earth, find me guilty, I will leave my innocent blood on them."* His statement caused a sensation among all present in the courtroom.

Redmond then stepped forward and stated: *"I am the murderer, not only of the Maddocks but of Roche, and he who stands by my side, as well as James Jackman, who was found guilty yesterday for the murder of Roche, are innocent. I am the murderer, and this man – pointing to Nicholas Jackman – is innocent. I have committed five murders with my own hands. I was put up to it all by bad persons – bad agents did it all. My poor father was turned out of his farm by a bad agent, because he wanted five pounds to make up his rent, although he had lived on it for upwards of sixty years."*

Judge Foster then sentenced the men to be hanged on the following Monday, 4 March. They were moved under a heavy armed escort back to the jail, where they were kept under a strong military guard until their execution.

The proprietor of *The Wexford Independent*, John Greene, was permitted to interview both men the next day, while they were held in their cells awaiting their fate. A devout Catholic and son of a Protestant mother, Elizabeth

Goodall, Greene was an active supporter of Daniel O'Connell and a firm opponent of violence. The Catholic Emancipation Act was passed just four years earlier in 1829 and this led to Wexford Corporation admitting, for the first time, 367 new freemen, most of them Catholic, including John Greene. He launched *The Wexford Independent* in December 1830. The liberal newspaper was a great success and was called simply *The Independent* from 1843 and later *The County Wexford Independent*. Greene was elected Mayor of Wexford seven times and later appointed a Justice of the Peace.

When John Greene entered the cell of Nicholas Jackman, the condemned man fell to his knees and protested his innocence. He *'called on Him who knows the secrets of all hearts, to witness the truth of what he said.'* John Redmond on the other hand told Greene that *'he was not sorry for what he did, and if he had the power he would commit the same deeds over again – that he would as soon die then as a month hence, as life had no charms for him – he got the retribution he desired for the wrongs, as he alleged, inflicted on his father.'*

The next day both men were taken to the gallows, a wooden structure erected on the green a few yards from the prison entrance. Jackman again declared his innocence. He knelt and prayed fervently and became so overcome that he had to be carried to the scaffold. Redmond again acknowledged his guilt but declared Jackman innocent before they were both hanged in front of an assembled crowd of onlookers.

A year after the hangings, some outbuildings on the Maddock farm were set alight. Labourers they employed were intimidated and the family continued to be threatened.

Redmond and Jackman were publicly hanged on gallows erected on the jail green outside Wexford Jail on Spawell Road in 1833. They were executed for the murders of three people, including a policeman, in revenge for the eviction of Redmond's family in Tomfarney.

Duncormick soldier was the 'Angel of Mons' in WWI

'The Angels of Mons' painted by William Margetson. Right: Sgt. Thomas Fitzpatrick during WWI.

THOMAS FITZPATRICK was born in Duncormick in 1879 to Thomas and Anastasia (née Connolly). He was the eldest of five children and his father was a member the Royal Irish Constabulary, assigned to Duncormick Station. In 1887 the family were living in Galbally and from 1893 Thomas Senior was sergeant in charge of the barracks in Tagoat until his retirement.

Young Thomas was educated at St. Aidan's Academy in Enniscorthy. The school was established 'to neutralise the Model School just established there', according to the *Kilkenny People*. The Model Schools were set up across the country in 1834-54 as mixed-denominational schools but were boycotted by the Catholic clergy, who wanted their own schools. Thomas was 18 in 1897 when he left the Academy and immediately joined the Royal Irish Regiment. Based in Victoria Barracks in Clonmel, the regiment recruited from counties Tipperary, Kilkenny, Waterford and Wexford. This was the start of an extraordinary 52-year career in the British Army, in which he survived two world wars, received 14 foreign decorations and was to rise to the rank of Lieutenant Colonel.

Thomas was dispatched to the North-East Frontier on the India and Afghanistan border (now part of Pakistan) within a year of joining the regiment. In 1904, he married Maud Wagner from Clonakilty, Co. Cork and the couple settled in Cork City. They had three children, Thomas, Maudie and Joseph and he was now stationed in Fermoy Barracks. He was appointed quartermaster sergeant, with responsibility for ensuring his unit was clothed and fed.

When World War I broke out in Europe in July 1914, Thomas was almost 35 and was again sent into a war zone, this time to the battlefields of Belgium and France, as part of the British Expeditionary Force. Germany had declared war on France on 3 August and crossed the border into Belgium the following day as their enormous war machine headed towards Paris. Britain felt obliged to uphold Belgium's neutrality, guaranteed in the 1839 Treaty of London. Orders to mobilize were received in the barracks in Clonmel on 4 August to ship out to Plymouth and then on by train to Southampton. Thomas embarked, along with the 2nd Royal Irish Regiment and escorted by ten cruisers, for Boulogne on board the *SS Hersche* on 14 August.

Just nine days later on Sunday 23 August 1914, the first major engagement of the war between British and German forces occurred outside the old Belgian coal-mining town of Mons, about ten miles from the French border.

On 22 August, the French Fifth Army was engaging the German First Army who were advancing towards France, in the Battle of Charleroi, east of Mons. The British reached Mons that day and agreed to hold the line along the Mons-Condé Canal for twenty-four hours in order to prevent the advancing Germans from surrounding the French forces. The canal ran through what was then an important coal-mining area surrounded by slag heaps and it was the intention of the British to hold the Germans on the northern side of the canal. The 2nd Royal Irish Regiment formed part of the 8th infantry brigade of the 3rd division of the British Army, totaling about 4,000 men. Some had fought together in the Boer War and in India but Thomas was a quartermaster and not a frontline soldier.

There was a semicircular bend in the canal at the village of Nimy and their task was to protect this section. The regiment defending Nimy Bridge was under intense gunfire and there were heavy casualties on both sides. In command of one machine-gun section was 24-year-old Lieutenant Maurice

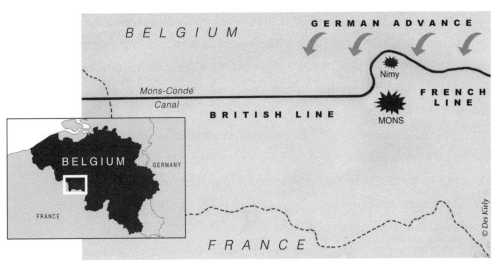

The British Expeditionary Force attempted to hold the line along the Mons-Condé Canal in support of the French 5th Army against the advancing German 1st Army at the Battle of Mons, 23 August 1914.

Dease from Coole, Co. Westmeath on his first day of combat. With most of his company dead or injured, he was wounded five times until he was finally carried away. He died that day from his wounds and was posthumously awarded the Victoria Cross for extreme bravery, the first recipient of the medal in World War I.

The British, though heavily outnumbered by about 3 to 1, succeeded in holding back the German advance. In order to avoid encirclement, however, the British had to finally retreat, leaving the canal line in German hands. But the British soldiers were dismayed at being ordered to retreat, having gained the upper hand against such odds. Only at the canal bend at Nimy had the Germans penetrated the British line of defence. By evening the Germans had overrun Mons to the east and occupied the town and were now threatening the rear area as well as the British line of retreat. There was now a risk of encirclement, complete annihilation or capture. Half of the entire British forces in Europe would be surrounded and the war at an end before it had even begun.

At La Bascule crossroads in the eastern suburbs of Mons, Sergeant Fitzpatrick had been told to await orders at around midday. He and about 50 men consisting of army cooks, storemen, drivers and delivery men were preparing a meal, having just been served beer in the Segard café. He could see his regiment were engaged by the Germans, coming under heavy machine-gun fire and some were in retreat. Thomas ordered his men to occupy a trench on the far side of the crossroads. From there they had a clear line of sight of the German advance. In front of them lay a British machine gun and the gunner lay dead beside it. Fitzpatrick and two others went, under fire, and recovered it. Now, as the German soldiers approached, they were gunned down by Thomas and his comrades.

Writing of the incident in 1955 in *The Old Contemptible,* a magazine for ex-servicemen, Thomas recalled that "everyone was now in good form and in good spirits," as if they were on a grouse hunt. "We felt we were on top of the world and had repulsed the whole German Army." But only 17 of the 50 men who fought with him in the trench that day survived.

By night-time the shooting had stopped, his men having held off the enemy for a full 11 hours. Stumbling over the bodies of about 50 German soldiers that they had killed, Thomas and his comrades went in search of their commander Captain Fergus Forbes, Earl of Granard, from Co. Longford. He was a half-brother of Lady Adelaide FitzGerald of Johnstown Castle. But they returned when they learned that he had been killed on the day. The Germans suffered heavy losses and when a group of German medical officers in a large

British infantry on the streets of Mons, surrounded by slag heaps, as they await the approach of the German 1st Army in what would be the first clash between British and German forces in World War 1.

Mercedes approached their trench, they demanded to be given access to the German injured. One of the German officers observed the Royal Irish badges. "I presume you must all be Ulstermen," he asked. Fitzpatrick was amused. "This remark was received by my men with hoots of derision. Lydon said he was from Wexford, others shouted their various counties, Waterford, Cork, Tipperary, Kerry, etc and I said jokingly, 'don't give information to the enemy'."

Thomas was almost 35 when he was dispatched to the battlefields of France and Belgium at the outbreak of WWI in 1914. (City of Mons Collection).

At about 11pm, Thomas and the surviving men buried their dead comrades in the trench where they had been killed. They then made their way to the British line to begin the retreat from Mons the next day with the German Army in pursuit. British casualties at Mons were around 1,600 killed and wounded with the 2nd Royal Irish Regiment suffering about 350 casualties. It is thought that more than 2,000 German troops were killed and wounded.

Mons is known as the 'the place of the first and the last' because the first British soldier to die in the conflict, John Parr, was killed here in 1914 and the last soldier, George Price, a Canadian, was shot dead in Mons by a German sniper, just three minutes before the church bells of the town rang out, announcing the armistice on 11 November 1918.

'ANGEL OF MONS'

Because the heavily-outnumbered British Army had managed to hold off the Germans at Mons for so long before being forced to retreat, the Battle of Mons became a remarkable morale booster back in Britain and army recruitment shot up in the weeks that followed.

Inspired by accounts that he had read of the fighting at Mons, Welsh author Arthur Machen wrote a short story entitled *The Bowmen*, a tale of supernatural intervention. It was published on the front page of *The London Evening News* on 29 September 1914 and because he wrote it from a first-hand perspective, many readers believed it to be true. The story was about the retreating British soldiers and how angels with bows and arrows had thrown a protective curtain around them, halted the German troops and so saved them from disaster. The story went viral in Britain and around the world. The popular version of the story was that it was angels who had stopped the evil Germans from advancing. Tales of the 'Angels of Mons' had entered the realms of legend and have persisted to this day.

More stories followed in the British press from 'anonymous British army officers' with such claims as that corpses of dead German soldiers found at Mons had been pierced by arrow wounds from the angels. Soldiers themselves began to bring back reports of heavenly interventions. It is believed that these stories were part of a covert attempt by the British War Office to spread morale-boosting propaganda. Some churches turned in favour of the war as a result, believing that these angels were a direct sign that God was on the British side. The story is still believed by many to be true.

As recently as 2001, an article in *The Sunday Times* claimed that a diary, film and photographic evidence proving the existence of the Angels of Mons from a World War I soldier named William Doidge had been found in a trunk in an antique shop. The story was picked up by newspapers and news media around the world. But the following year it was admitted that the story was a complete hoax; neither the footage nor the soldier ever existed.

Visitors to the city of Mons in search of the origins of the 'Angel of Mons' story are directed to La Bascule crossroads where a three-metre high Celtic cross was

Memorial at La Bascule crossroads in Mons to Sergeant Thomas Fitzpatrick and the 2nd Royal Irish Regiment, who were recruited mainly from counties Tipperary, Kilkenny, Waterford and Wexford.

erected in 1923 by the people of Mons. It commemorates Sergeant Thomas Fitzpatrick from Duncormick and the men of the 2nd Royal Irish Regiment, who delayed the German advance and so protected the British retreat. The memorial was unveiled on 11 November 1923, the 5th anniversary of Armistice Day, by Field Marshal John French, Commander-in-Chief of the British Expeditionary Force. In his speech in French he said: "Years must pass before the true history of the Great War can be known and understood, but when this moment comes the attitude of the soldiers of Ireland will stand out nobly. They were always where the fighting was hottest and the Irish regiments held their ground with a tenacity that has never been surpassed."

For his gallantry at the Battle of Mons, Thomas Fitzpatrick received the Distinguished Conduct Medal (DCM) from the British Government, the Medaille Militaire from the French (their equivalent of the Victoria Cross) and the Order of St. George from Russia.

A few weeks after retreating from Mons, the 2nd Royal Irish Regiment suffered a catastrophe at the French hamlet of Le Pilly in Herlies in northern France on 19 October. The 904 young men found themselves isolated from their division and surrounded by German troops, who shelled and machine-gunned them. Some 170 were killed and 302 taken prisoner. The names of many of the 27 Wexford men who died on the day appear in the archive www.wexfordgreatwardead.ie Only the remains of eight have a grave. Somewhere in French Flanders lie the bodies of the other 162 Irishmen. The following year Thomas nearly died after being gassed and taken to hospital in Boulogne. The regiment would be virtually wiped out four times throughout the First World War.

In 1926, Thomas joined the Egyptian Police of Alexandria and Cairo. During the Second World War he was chief of police in the Suez Canal area of Egypt during the North Africa campaign between the Allies and Italy and Germany for control of the vital waterway linking the West and the East. He later became Honorary Observer of the Egyptian Royal Air Force and was recalled to the regular British Army in 1946. Thomas continued in uniform until his retirement as Lieutenant Colonel in 1949, having served in the British Army for 52 years. The 'Angel of Mons' died in a London nursing home in 1965, aged 84.

The magic of Yoletown Farm: recipe for a stable lifestyle

The striking two-storey thatched farmhouse and enclosed courtyard at Yoletown near Tacumshane.

KATHERINE CARROLL first visited the distinct two-storey whitewashed thatched farmhouse in Yoletown, located between Tacumshane and Lady's Island Lake, as a five-year-old child in 1959. This was the home of her beloved Aunt Kitty. Today, Katherine is the custodian of the nearly 300-year-old farm, which has always been a place of magic and healing for her and where twenty-five years ago she established the highly successful wholefood business *Stable Diet*.

The name Yoletown (*ye old town*) derives from the Yola (*old*) dialect, spoken here in the barony of Forth, as well as the adjoining barony of Bargy, following the Anglo-Norman invasion in 1169 up to the mid-1800s. Baldwin Keating, a descendant of the Anglo-Norman FitzGeralds, is believed to have built Baldwinstown Castle in about 1210. His brother, Robert Keating is recorded as Lord of Slievecoiltia in 1200. The Keatings, one of the principal families colonizing south Wexford, were also granted Kilcowan in Bargy. A more recent member of the clan was Pat Keating, who inherited Yoletown Farm from his mother Maria, his father John having died when Pat was a schoolboy, while his brother entered the priesthood. When in his early sixties, Pat married 37-year-old Christina Cummins (Kitty) in 1957. Kitty had grown up on Waterloo Road in Wexford town and worked as a nurse. When she moved into Yoletown, where she was to spend the rest of her life, she gave up her nursing career and became part of the very structured, tight-knit Keating family. A relatively young Kitty now shared the house with her husband and his two spinster sisters, May and Bab.

Kitty's brother Andy Cummins farmed in Danescastle, Carrick-on-Bannow and was married to Nora (née Moynihan). They had five children and the eldest was Katherine. The fondest childhood memories that Katherine has are their family visits to Uncle Pat and Aunty Kitty in the Keating family farm at Yoletown in the 1950s and '60s. Her father would drive their Hillman van the 25 miles from Danescastle to Yoletown, often having to stop at the railway crossing at Bridgetown as the steam train passed on the now defunct Rosslare-Waterford line. Andy and his sister Kitty had a close relationship and so the family visited Yoletown every few weeks, especially in summer when they could stay longer and enjoy the bright evenings. On arrival, they were greeted by Kitty, Pat's sisters May and Bab and the housekeeper, Katie Furlong. If Uncle Pat was not busy on the farm, he would be there to welcome them too.

The entire Keating family in front of the Thatch, c.1900. Maria and John Keating and their children Babs (on nanny's lap), May, Mordie and Pat. (photo: Charles E. Vize)

The main house is a two-storey thatch, always referred to simply as the Thatch. Its courtyard enclosure they call the Yard is surrounded by farm buildings, some of which were originally also thatched. The Thatch has very thick, solid, mud and stone walls, but no foundations in the conventional sense. There are no windows at either gable end and only a tiny one upstairs at the back. A water pump still stands dutifully in the middle of the Yard with a stone trough underneath.

'Even back during those early visits, and without fully understanding it, I felt a remarkable sense of natural abundance and lushness embracing and infusing Yoletown and its environs', says Katherine. *'Even when I grew into my teens it maintained its magnetic pull for me.'*

Katherine loved the farming life. As a child on their family visits to Yoletown she enjoyed spending time with the cows Daisy and Bess, as they munched on vegetable peelings from the kitchen while Bab hand-milked them in the cow-house that is still part of the Yard. The resident peacock fascinated her with his colourful plumage and loud shrieks. However, the

Kitty and Pat haymaking together on Yoletown Farm.

giant shire horses were the biggest attraction and the highlight of the visit would be if she was allowed by Willie the farm worker to ride one of them back to the field by the duck pond after their day's work. The three women, Kitty, May and Bab, were all actively involved during haymaking and harvesting in the summertime and Katherine was only too happy to join in the work. *'Coming here for the day with the family was an exciting event in itself, so imagine how it was the first time I was allowed to stay over for a few days with my sister Marie'*, Katherine recalls.

Just a few fields away is the site of the annual pilgrimage, which starts on 15 August to the shrine of Our Lady's Island, an important date in the calendar. Uncle Pat played a prominent role in the ceremonies, carrying banners and other regalia. Afterwards, the farmhouse would be crowded with nuns and priests and family friends. Walking the pilgrimage path around the island with her parents is fondly remembered by Katherine. They would try to catch a glimpse of Yoletown Farm in the distance beyond the far side of the lake, as they turned at the head of the peninsula.

In March 1941, a German Luftwaffe plane, in an attack on a British cargo vessel off the Welsh coast, was hit by return gunfire. The crew chose to attempt to reach Ireland and crash-landed on Rostoonstown Strand, a broad stretch of beach that separates Lady's Island Lake from the sea. Having then blown up the plane, the crewmen were accompanied by Pat Keating and other locals to Tacumshane. There they were given refreshments before being arrested and taken to the military barracks in Wexford and transferred the next day to the Curragh Internment Camp. *(The full story is in Fascinating Wexford History, Volume One)*.

Katherine and her siblings attended Danescastle Primary School and when she was 12 she obtained a scholarship to Loreto Convent School in Wexford, the nearest town. The 20-mile journey to and from school would have been impossible back then and so boarding was her only option. Katherine found it hard to adjust and missed her family as well as the animals and farming activities. She pushed herself hard in her studies but after developing some health issues, left school aged 16. She started working again with her father on the farm while her mother resumed her teaching career.

In 1974, Katherine married Denis Carroll and they lived in a newly-built house on his father's land in Arnestown outside New Ross. Denis had a machinery business and Katherine worked on the accounts. They kept no animals and she was missing farm life. Their son Ross was born in 1976.

Both Pat and his brother Muredoch died in 1976. As well as losing her husband, Kitty also lost her sister Eilis that same year. Pat's sisters May and Bab and Kitty herself were in failing health. Katherine's father Andy worried about his sister Kitty and her heavy load of responsibilities. It was then that he suggested that Katherine might consider moving to Yoletown with her family to run the farm and support his sister in any way she could.

Andy had to first investigate Kitty's reaction to such a proposal. Having dropped a number of subtle hints, he found that the plan met with her careful approval. May and Bab thought it was a wonderful idea. Katherine's husband Denis could run his business from Yoletown and so they made the move in 1979, three years after the death of Pat. The very idea of living and working here was a hugely exciting prospect for Katherine. They lived in a caravan borrowed from a friend of Kitty's that they parked in the Yard. The following year they built a wooden house in what used to be a small orchard near the Thatch, the same cosy wooden house that Katherine still lives in today. Set among wild grass and buttercups and surrounded by trees and shrubs, it fits perfectly into the surroundings. *'My brother used to say that it looked as if the house had grown in the garden, which is a wonderful way of describing it,'* says Katherine.

When May died in 1982 and Bab in 1985, aged 85, it was the end of the Keating line in Yoletown. Katherine's father Andy, who had been Katherine's rock throughout her life, died suddenly in 1984. Denis and Katherine's second son Steven was born in 1985.

Kitty remained living in the Thatch, now pursuing an independent life of her own. There was a government scheme that allowed for somebody who did not have children, such as Kitty, to pass on a farm to someone who had worked on it for at least five years, giving them official tax status equivalent to

The very popular award-winning Stable Diet café on Wexford's South Main Street.

a son or daughter. That's precisely how Katherine came to inherit the farm in 1985. It must have been a big step for Kitty, signing across her home and the farm, but leaving her with a right of residence for her lifetime.

In as far back as the early 1800s, tobacco was cultivated in the Wexford area. Crops were grown in Yoletown between 1908 and 1913 and overseen by Pat's widowed mother, Maria Keating. Pat took up tobacco-growing again in 1932 in the field still known as the Tobacco Field. The crop was then taken to a curing barn in nearby Broadway. One day, shortly after Kitty's death in 2012, while exploring a shelf over the range in the kitchen, Katherine found a tin labelled 'Orinoco half acre' containing 90-year-old tobacco seeds.

The years passed and with a worsening back problem, Katherine had to move away from the heavy manual work of the farm. She can trace her fascination with cooking back to her childhood in Danescastle. Watching her mother baking scones, apple tarts, brown bread, white bread and currant bread left a lasting impression on her. After leaving school, she tried her hand at baking and discovered a whole new world.

Katherine has always loved cookery books as much as she loves cooking.

In a sideboard in the Thatch, Katherine found a box of these old labels for jars of apple jam that were produced on the farm, long before Stable Diet.

Starting with a small bakery in the garden, she established the brand *Stable Diet* in 1995, supplying carrot cake and breads to the health store Only Natural in Wexford town. The business expanded slowly but surely, soon producing 300 loaves of brown bread each day. It was hard work for Katherine and one assistant, taking all day to produce cakes and scones and

Katherine baking bread in the evenings.

Vincent Power, who farmed next door to Yoletown Farm, became involved in the business and soon a bigger production unit was underway. The building was completed in 1999 and a new driveway and entrance were created. The following year, Katherine began the restoration of the outbuildings in the Yard and workshops covering meditation, yoga, aromatherapy and alternative lifestyles were held, all with Kitty's approval too. Some of the buildings were adapted as apartments for those running or attending the workshops. Later the accommodation was rented out on a permanent basis, often to some who had come to work in the bakery.

Over the past twenty five years, *Stable Diet* has produced wholefood breads, preserves, chutneys, cakes, sauces, dressings, biscuits, oat flapjacks and cereals that appeared on the shelves of stores and cafés around Ireland. All their food products are handmade, mostly wheat free and based on traditional recipes using natural ingredients. They have won numerous awards over the years and remain true to their philosophy: nature knows best.

An article in *Ireland of the Welcomes* magazine in 2002 described Katherine and her love of animals: *Katherine is something of a healer, a restorer, herself; a finder of the lost black lamb (so small she thought it was a blackbird), her fields give sanctuary for the broken-down racehorse which lives with his companionable sheep, to the foundling pony which produced a foal, to a pair of mislaid deer, a few donkeys and several ostriches which were just left off a trailer by strangers in her yard. Even the dovecote in the yard*

Katherine Carroll ponders at the window of her house on Yoletown Farm. (photo: Nadia Michnik)

has been home to an unexpected family of kittens.

Today, *Stable Diet* products continue to be sold countrywide and the very popular Stable Diet café in Wexford opened in 2007. The café has won many awards over the years and is known for its friendly staff and ambience. As Katherine says 'We put our heart in what we do.'

For thirty-three years, Katherine shared Yoletown Farm with Kitty, who passed away in her 92nd year in 2012. The Thatch is undergoing some restoration as dry rot appeared after the house was left unoccupied for a short time. Katherine is hoping it will be lived in again, perhaps by herself one day, as Kitty probably would have wanted.

(Extracts from 'The Energy of Place: the Magic of Yoletown Farm' by Katherine Carroll).

Between Yoletown Farm and Lady's Island Lake stands the ruin of a fortified house in the adjoining townland of Rathshillane. Not a tower house but a three-storey heavily protected house, with fifteen gun-loops on the ground floor. The structure was first mentioned in 1616, when it was held by Robert French. Nearby Ballytory Castle was the principal stronghold of the prominent French family. Nicholas French, born at Ballytory, was appointed Catholic bishop of Ferns in 1646 but forced to flee to Spain in 1651 following the Cromwellian invasion.

Rathshillane, a heavily fortified house, once the home of the French family. (photo: Nadia Michnik)

Sir William Brereton's account of a visit to Wexford in 1634

The English politician Sir William Brereton (1604-1661).

SIR WILLIAM BRERETON was a Member of Parliament for Cheshire from 1628 in the reign of Charles I until the following year when the King decided to rule without parliament for the next eleven years. When the English Civil War broke out in 1642, Brereton joined the Parliamentarian forces and became army Commander-in-Chief for Cheshire. Seven years later, the Parliamentarians would execute Charles I.

In Ireland, Anglicism had been declared the state religion and lands were confiscated by English and Scottish settlers in the plantations of Munster and Ulster in the 16th and 17th century. This enforced colonization of the country eventually led to the Confederate Wars in 1641 between the Catholic gentry and the Protestant and Presbyterian planters. Finally, in 1649 Oliver Cromwell arrived to settle matters.

Fifteen years before Cromwell's sack of Wexford town, William Brereton visited the area and kept a detailed record in a diary of a journey that he made through County Wexford nearly 400 years ago. In the summer of 1634, he landed in Ireland in the company of two other would-be colonists, a Mr.

Plummer and a Mr. Needham, with the intention of acquiring land in the troubled country. They travelled from Enniscorthy to Wexford and from there to Tintern Abbey, where they lodged for two nights with the Colcloughs. They then continued to Ballyhack and by ferry to Passage. Brereton made reference to rebel activity in the New Ross area that forced them to alter their route as they headed for Waterford. He observed how women in Wexford dressed and he used some peculiar spellings for placenames such as Wexford, which was spelt thus in the period. This is the extract from Brereton's diary:

"Ennerscottie, July 10.–We went hence towards Washiforde [Wexford], which is accounted 8 miles, butt they are very long miles. We crossed the river at Ennerscottie on horseback, and at the Carrick, a mile from Washiforde, we passed over a narrow ferrie. Still, the grass in the countrye is burned uppe, and here they complain of drought, and affirm they never felt such intense scortching hott weather in Ireland.

Here are divers of the Roches, which have much lande about Washiforde, and who would willingly sett or sell. Their lande lyeth very convenient for a Cheshireman. About a mile hence lies a farme called the "Parke", which is now leased unto one Mr. Hardey, an Englishman, who lives upon itt, and

Ferrycarrig and Roche's tower house before the construction of the bridge. From a sketch by the Dutch-born artist Gabriel Beranger, who had a print shop on South Great George's Street, Dublin. (National Library of Ireland)

hath an estate in itt about 13 years. The Landlord is one Mr. William Synode [Sinnott], of the Lough [Garrylough], a man in neede of money. This land is almost an Islande, and the rent which Mr. Hardey payes is about £16 a yeare. Hee saith itt contains about 300 acres, others say 200 acres, and that itt will keep 30 milch kine [cows], and yield sufficient corne for a small familey. Itt affordes abundance of rabbits, whereof there are soe many, soe they pester the ground—and here may be more fish and fowle provided than to keepe a good familey—for on 3 sides itt is compassed with great Loughes, a mile or two broade, soe as the floode being in, itt flowes to the verye bank-sides—when the floode is out the shoare is muddie, bare and drie. The depth of the mudde is half a yarde, or a yarde, butt I could not finde the mudde bare, and this was the reason given by Mr. Hardey, that soe long as the wind blows west, itt cleares itt of water—butt now the wind being at east, keepes the tyde in. When the flood is in, itt is said to be nott above 1 yd. deepe of water (except at some extraordinary spring-tydes.) I cannott believe butt that this mudde will much fertilize, and enrich the ground. This I do believe is a place of much securitie for cattle or goodes, as are therein kept, and this they affirme that they have nott lost any since they came thither, which is about 8 years.

Here is the best feeding for fowle that I ever saw—this grass which comes from the mudde is good foode for them, and there is a good store of itt :—and here is a little grove of oakes, wherein is no good timber, butt, itt soe stands as itt is most strong shelter for the fowle that feede or frequent under itt. Here is the most commodious and convenient seate for a Castle that ever I saw, butt there is no more roame whereuppon to erect a Castle betwixt the water and the high bank of the woode, than 4 or 5 roode in breadth, but sufficient in length : so as you must either make soe muche of the mudde firm lande, whereuppon to build your Castle, or else you must only make good one side with two pipes, or you must erect your worke upon a pointe of lande which lyeth much eastwarde, and is in view of the towne, and much more inconvenient, or must carry away abundance of earth to make pond and pipes in some grounde yett much too high at the north-west end of the woode. Here grow Ollers sufficient to plant a coy, and here is sufficient wood to cleave into stakes for all uses :—and as I am informed, reeds may be provided out of Sir Thomas Esmond's land which is on the other side of the water, and all necessaries may be supplied by water from the Slane.

Mr. Hardey demands for his interest, which is for 13 years, £55, and will not abate anything. Herein grow good cherries, and all wood planted flourisheth well. Mr. Turner, father-in-law to Mr. William Synode, demanded an £100 fine for a lease of 80 years in reversion, after the determination of the 13 years now in being—of the unreasonableness of which demanding convinced, he sent next day a message and a letter to his son-in-law, who desired to know what I would give, I would offer nothing—butt Mr. Mainwaring offered £20 for a lease for 80 years. Mr. Turner replied that £40 would not be accepted, whereuppon this wee breake off.

We lodged at Washiforde, at the sign of the "Windmill," att the house of Paul Bennett.

Washiforde.—This towne is seated uppon a brave spacious harbour, capacious of many 100 sayle, butt itt is much prejudiced and damnified by a most vile barred haven, which notwithstanding, is better that formerly. Two narrowe bankes of sand runne along on both sides of the Channell, or passage. Trade much decayeth in this towne, and itt is very poore, by reason of the Hearring-fishery here failing. They report here an incredible multitude of Hearrings ordinarily taken in one night, in this vaste and large harbour, by 5 or 6 men in one boate of ten tuns burden; sometimes to the value of £20, sometimes £30, sometimes £40, sometimes more. This was affirmed me by one that ordinarily fished here, and tooke this proportion. Now of later times the Hearrings having forsaken the coast, this towne is much impoverished and decayed, their keyes goe to ruine, and are in noe good repaire.—There belonged sometimes unto every great merchant's house seated on the shoare, either a key, or a part interest in a key, or a private way to the key. Their haven was then furnished with 500 sayle of shippes, and small vessels for fishing, and is now naked.

July 18.–This day I went to the Court, (the Assizes being now held here for this County of Washiforde, which began on Wednesday last, and ended this day,) where is the Shire-Hall. The Judges that ride this circuite, are Sir George Shirley, Lord Chiefe Justice of Irelande, and Sir John Phillpott, one of the Judges of Common Pleas, a little black, temperate man. The one, viz., my Lord Chiefe Justice, sitts uppon Nisi Prins–the other uppon matters of misdemeanours, and trials for life and death. Here I saw 4 Justices of Peace uppon the bench with Sir John Phillpott, among which was one Devereux and

From a map of Ireland drawn and engraved by the Flemish cartographer Gerardus Mercator (1512-1594). It was published by his sons Rumold & Henricus as an atlas, after his death, in 1595. This detail shows Wexford County (Weyshford Comitatus) bordering with Dublin County, before the creation of the county of Wicklow.

my cousin Mainwaring, unckle to Mr. Mainwaring that now is ; a courteous, grave, civill, gentleman, who came from the bench and saluted mee in the hall, and accompanied mee to the taverne, and bestowed wine uppon mee. He is agent for Sir Henry Walloppe [who had Enniscorthy Castle built in its present form], and is a Justice of the Peace for the Countey, and was a Burgess of the Parliament.

He told me there were three Rebells condemned, as alsoe, he advised mee, rather to goe by Ballihack, and by the way of the Passage, than by Ross, because of the rebells which frequent thereabouts. Hereof, hee said, there were about 6 or 8, and these furnished with some pieces, pistolls, darts and skenes, and some of them most desperate spirrits, and soe cruell that the inhabitants of the countrie dare scarce travell that way. These are proclaymed rebells, and as such are to be hanged, drawn and quartered, soe soon as they are apprehended–soe, alsoe, are those to be dealt with who are now to be executed. One of them I saw in the streets returning towards the Castle, and the women and some others following, making lamentation, sometimes soe violent, as though they were distracted, and sometimes as itt were a kind of tone singing. One of these ('twas said) was his wife. This is the Irish garb here.

This towne is governed by a Maior and 2 Bayliffes, or Sheriffes, and 10 or 12 Aldermen. Beyonde the Barre alsoe, itt hath a very safe harbour, and shelter

121

for shippes to ride at anchor in, who want tide to bringe them into the haven. Sir Adam Cotoliffe [Colclough] told mee that he had dined at Milford, in Wales, and supped in this towne, which is about 24 hours sayle from Bristoll, and as much from Dublin.

By reason of the Assizes here, the inhabitants of the countrie resorted hither in greater numbers and better habbitts (Irish garments I mean,) than I have yett seen.–Some gentlewomen of good qualitie, I observed clothed in good handsome gownes, petticoates and hatts, who wore Irish rugges which have handsome, comelie large fringes, which goe aboute their neckes, and serve instead of bandes. This rugg-fringe is joined to a garment which comes round about them, and reacheth to the very grounde, and thus is a handsome comelie vestment, much more comelie as they are used, than the rugg short cloakes used by the women uppon festivall dayes in Abbeville, Bullen, and the nearer parts of Picardie, in France.

The most of the women are bare-necked and clean-skinned, and weare a Crucifix, tied in a black necklace hanging betwixt their breasts–itt seems they are not ashamed of their religion, nor desire to conceal themselves–and, indeed, in this towne there are many Papists. The present Maior, Mr. Mark Chevey [Cheevers], attended the Judges to the Church doore, and soe did the Sheriffe of the Shire, both which left them there, and went to Mass, which is tolerated here, and publiquely resorted to in 3 or 4 houses in this towne, wherein are very few Protestants, as appeared by that slender congregation at Church where the Judges were.

This morning I went unto and visited both Judges, and was respectfully used by them. The Maior, a well-bred gentleman that hath an estate in the countrie, and was Knight of the Shire for the last Parliament, invited mee to dinner, as alsoe to supper with the Judges. He is an Irishman, and his wife Irish, in a strange habbitt, with thread-bare shorte coate with sleeves made like my green coate of stuffe, reaching to her middle. She knew nott how to carve, looke, entertaine, or demeane herself.–Here was a kind of beere, (which I durst not taste) called Charter Beere, mighty thicke, muddie stuffe– the meale nothing well cooqued nor ordered.

Much discourse here–complaint and information given against the Rebells, the Captaine whereof is called Simon Prendergast, whose brother alsoe will be brought to trouble. Three carriers were robbed between Ross and this towne, on Friday last, and 2 other travellers, and one in his lodging, by three of these rebells, well appointed, who said, if they had taken my Lord Kildare, who passed through them nakedly, unattended, he should have prayed their pardon.

There was a letter sent and reade this night att the supper, advertising a gentleman in towne, that last night they came to his house with a purpose to take away his life, because hee prosequted against them, and informed that they had taken from him to the value of £200. The Judges here said, if the Juctices of the Peace did nott waite

Sir Adam Colclough (1600-1637), who provided board to Brereton and his companions at his residence, Tintern Abbey, for two nights in July, 1634.

uppon them to Ross, to guard them from these rebells, he would fine them deeply. The junior Judge told mee of a verie wise demean of the now Maior of Ross, who being informed that three of these rebells lay asleepe neere the towne, and being required to send out some 10 or 12 with him to apprehend them, he assured that he would provide for the safetye of his towne— he commanded the gates to be shutt, the drumme to be beaten, and warning pieces to be discharged, wherebye they awaked, and so took notice thereof, and escaped.

July 20.–We left Washiforde and the Lord provided a good guide for us, and directed us to a better course than wee intended, for instead of going over the Passage (which was this day soe much troubled and soe roughe, as my Lord Kildare was in great danger there, and himself and his servaunts constrained to cutt the sail-ropes and jack-lines), wee took upp our lodging att Tinterden [Tintern] a dissolved Abbey, where now Sir Adam Cotoliffe [Colclough] lives, and where wee were exceedingly kindly and courteouslie entertained. This is a verie long statelie house, and of good receipt–adjoining the Abbey which is still in good repair, and Sir Adam keepes a good, hospitable boarde, well supplyed and attended, and is to all a most warm-hearted and courteous gentleman. Wee stayed two dayes here until the storm abated, when we left him, highly gratified for his kind entertainment, and passing over the Passage, proceeded to Waterford."

Exorcism in Killinick caused the death of a child

photo: Wesley Almeida

CATHERINE SINNOTT was three-and-a-half years old when local curate Father John Carroll attempted to perform an exorcism on her in 1824. The little girl died as a result and the priest, along with five of his parishioners, were put on trial for her murder.

Killinick was at the time accessible by cot, a flat-bottomed sailing vessel, from Wexford Harbour. But the South Slobs were created in the mid-1800s, when mudflats stretching from Drinagh to Killinick were reclaimed from the sea, making the village landlocked. From Lewis's 1837 *Topographical Dictionary of Ireland* description of Killinick: 'Coal and other commodities are brought up in cots from Wexford harbour, by an inlet which is navigable at spring tides. Some of the inhabitants on the banks of this inlet are engaged in fishing. Fairs are held in the village...petty sessions are held every fortnight or month, on Tuesdays, and here is a constabulary police station.'

Father John Carroll, described as tall and of a striking appearance, from the townland of Ballysheen, Killinick, was a curate in the parish for several years. He was held in high regard by the community. Many parishioners believed that he possessed superior powers over other priests and could work miracles. It was claimed that a parishioner by the name of Peg Furlong, who appeared to be dead, was prayed over by Father Carroll, who then shook her and she recovered.

According to witness statements in the subsequent court case for the murder of Catherine Sinnott, the following distressing events occurred in Killinick on 9 July 1824:

Mrs. Neal, an elderly widow in the village, was ill and bedridden for a long time and it was believed that Father Carroll cured her that day. He was also credited with performing an exorcism on a man in her home on the same day. There was a large number of neighbours present in the house when Father Carroll went outside and was seen pacing up and down on the road. A neighbour, Mrs. Moran, was lying speechless on the roadway. The priest was seen to stop near her. He stamped his foot twice on the ground and cried out 'Begone!' He then spat two or three times in her direction, threw himself onto his back and then proceeded to rub the back of his hand on the gravel, causing it to bleed. A number of people were kneeling and watching what was going on. Father Carroll then got up and again and paced up and down the road. Standing over Mrs. Moran, he said in a loud voice, 'Jesus, Jesus, Jesus! Father, Father, Father, assist me!' while at the same time moving his hand over her body.

The priest, with arms extended, continued on to the house of Thomas Sinnott, about 200 yards away, and a large number of the crowd followed.

The curate, Father John Carroll.

He entered the house uninvited, and went into a room off the kitchen where little Catherine was lying in bed. The child suffered from fits and the belief was that she was possessed by evil spirits. The little girl was crying out: 'Oh Daddy Daddy, Oh Mammy Mammy, save me!' Father Carroll proceeded to sit on the girl and then jump on her as she screamed out in pain. He then stood on the bed with his hands raised. He ordered that a tub of water be brought in and placed on the bed. He then recited some words in Latin and threw a handful of salt into the water and poured some over the child. The priest then flipped the tub over with his foot, spilling in over the bed. He said in a loud voice: 'Bury him, Jesus, in the depth of the sea.' He then sat on the tub and said: 'Bury him, Jesus, in the depth of the Red Sea.'

The tub was now lying upside-down on top of the little girl with the priest sitting on it. He then stood on the tub and began jumping on it. As he leapt he was shouting 'Jesus, Jesus, Jesus! Father, Father, Father!' The child's mother was present in the room for the entire time. The priest then sat on the tub repeating the words and remained sitting in that position for at least three hours. At one stage he whistled a hornpipe while keeping time by tapping his foot.

One of the men present, William Furlong, a close friend of the family, told the child's mother and her brother James that the priest was mad. He asked somebody in the room to fetch three other priests from the parish because he believed Father Carroll was insane. But nobody went for help or intervened to stop the priest. A passage through the crowd was left clear to allow the devil to pass from the child and out the front door of the house. One of the men in the room, Patrick Parel, advised Furlong to 'keep out of the way, as the devil was going to be expelled from the child, and that it might hurt him in passing out'.

The girl's father, Thomas Sinnott, arrived at the house after the priest had already begun the exorcism. As he approached his daughter's bed, people in the house told him to be quiet and to kneel down like them as the priest was going to perform a miracle. Everybody knelt and prayed.

Three hours passed before it became apparent that the little girl was dead. Thomas Sinnott lifted the child's body from the bed and held her to the priest, who instructed him to lay her down again. Sinnott believed that Father Carroll would bring the child back to life. But the priest told Sinnott that he should resign it to the will of God, and left. Little Catherine Sinnott lay dead on the bed. It was four o'clock in the morning when the priest mounted his horse and rode off at speed.

The next evening, Doctor Rennick attended Father Carroll, whom he believed was deranged. He restrained the priest and released blood from his temple artery. Bloodletting was used at the time to treat almost every disease and leeches were commonly used to withdraw blood. Bloodletting was normally carried out by barbers, and the red-and-white-striped pole of the barbershop, still in use today, is derived from this practice (the red symbolizes blood while the white symbolizes the bandages). But Father Carroll removed the dressings and so the doctor had to place handcuffs on him. The priest was raving and speaking about the devils that he had driven from the people.

The trial of Father Carroll and five of his parishioners, Nicholas Wickham, James Devereux, Patrick Parel, Nicholas Corrish and Walter Scallan was heard in Wexford Crown Court on 4 August 1824. The parishioners were accused of aiding and assisting in the murder of Catherine Sinnott. As he sat in the courtroom, Father Carroll appeared calm for the duration of the proceedings. His face was pale and his head wrapped in a bandage. During the testimony being given by the many witnesses on the events that led to the killing of the child, it was noted that the five parishioners were eating cherries.

Doctor Devereux from Wexford gave evidence of treating Father Carroll over the previous three years. He testified that he believed the witness was insane and that the parish priest was aware of his condition but Father Carroll had not been prevented from officiating in the parish. Doctor Devereux had prescribed medication, which the priest had stopped taking for the last two months. Early in the afternoon on the day in question he saw the priest looking dishevelled, sitting in a ditch with a number of people around him. He observed that he had the appearance of being deranged.

The trial caused a sensation in the county and beyond. When it ended, the jury retired for just a few minutes before returning with a verdict of not guilty on Father Carroll and all five parishioners. The priest was acquitted on account of being insane at the time of the killing. After the verdicts were read, the judge addressed those present: 'I hope that what has this day transpired in this court will teach the lower orders to distrust the promises of such professors – let them resort to the power of the Almighty in the only way in which he himself has pointed out, and that is by the exercise of prayer.' The justice concluded: 'John Carroll, you are to be detained in custody until the Lord Lieutenant's pleasure is known.' [The then Lord Lieutenant of Ireland was Richard Wellesley].

The incident and trial garnered wide publicity and outrage in Ireland and Britain. The child's father, and particularly her mother, were widely condemned for not protesting against her treatment and for their blind trust in the healing powers of the priest. Reports of the trial and the story of the murder were published in detail in the *Wexford Herald, The Freeman's Journal* – and in the *Belfast Newsletter* under the headline 'Horrible fanaticism and cruelty.' A booklet entitled: *Fanaticism! Cruelty!! Bigotry!!! The particulars of the horrible murder of Catharine Sinnott, a child under four years of age, by the Rev. John Carroll, an Irish Catholic priest, under pretence of performing a miracle, by casting devils out of the child, which took place at Killinick, in the County of Wexford, on Friday, July 9, 1824, etc.* was published by John Fairburn in London in 1824.

Official Catholic guidelines for exorcism were set out in 1614 and revised by the Vatican in 1999 with the publication of the booklet *De Exorcismis et Supplicationibus Quibusdam*. A potentially possessed individual must now first be evaluated by a medical professional to ascertain if the person is suffering from mental illness. The Vatican requires each diocese to have a trained exorcist available. *The Dark Sacrament,* co-written by Christina McKenna (this writer's sister-in-law) documents ten cases of exorcisms in modern Ireland.

She had her own experience of an exorcism as a girl aged eleven growing up in County Derry. After her great-aunt died she heard a continuous tapping sound under the bed where she had slept. Priests came and prayed but could not to stop it. An exorcist arrived from England and ended the presence in the house.

A famous County Wexford exorcism was performed in Loftus Hall on Hook Peninsula in late 1700s by the local parish priest Father Thomas Broaders. The legend of Loftus Hall tells the story of a visit by the Devil, which was followed by poltergeist activity for a number of years until Father Broaders successfully exorcised the house – except for the Tapestry room. *(See story on page 64).*

Levitation is thought to often be involved in cases of demonic possession. (photo: Des Kiely)

'You can't hang Wicklow men in Wexford!'

The old Wexford Jail, location of the last hanging in Wexford in 1892.

IN 1890, Daniel and James Handley, brothers from County Wicklow, were found guilty of the murder of shopkeeper Maryanne Lyons, a 65-year-old widow. The killing took place in the village of Barndarrig, located on the main road from Arklow to Wicklow. When it was announced that the young siblings were both to be hanged in Wexford there was a chorus of 'You can't hang Wicklow men in Wexford!'.

There were 16 murders recorded in Ireland in 1890, two of these in County Wicklow. In June, a 34-year-old dressmaker, Elizabeth Grundy, was shot dead in her shop in Delgany by a 'tramp painter'. He wished to marry her, but she did not return his affection. The accused was declared insane by a jury and ordered to be confined in a lunatic asylum. The second murder took place six months later, again in a shop, but this time in Barndarrig.

Mrs. Lyons ran a small grocery shop, the only source of provisions in the village of Barndarrig. The store was an extension to her cottage and was located in the heart of the village, close to Barndarrig Church. She was said to have had eccentric ways. There were whispers locally that she held a considerable sum of money in the house, on account of her preference for not opening the shop to customers after dark, unless they first knocked on the door. It later emerged that the elderly lady kept the bulk of her money in the safe custody of her friend, schoolteacher Elizabeth Thompson. She also held some cash inside a clock in her own sitting-room.

James Kehoe, a local villager, called to the shop late one evening in December 1890 to buy some tobacco. At his knock, the shop light went out and the door was not opened. Assuming Mrs. Lyons was going to bed, he called to his friends Daniel and James Handley. Neither was home and so he waited until they returned later that evening.

Daniel was married and about 20 years old and James was only 15. They came from Rathnew, close to Wicklow town and about seven miles north of Barndarrig. Both were employed in Barndarrig as labourers by a local farmer named Costelloe and lodged in his thatched farmhouse. The brothers were known to be involved in poaching locally.

The morning after Kehoe had called to the shop, Mrs. Lyons' friend Elizabeth Thompson dropped by and discovered her body lying on the bedroom floor of her cottage. Her head lay in a pool of blood. The house appeared to have been ransacked by the perpetrator and the motive was evidently robbery.

The police questioned six men who had been seen on the streets of Barndarrig the previous night. These included Kehoe and the Handley brothers. Kehoe related the events of the night and claimed that when the Handleys arrived home they both appeared to be in shock. James's clothes were wet although it had not been raining. Daniel had blood on his lips and told him, "I caught myself on a prickly shrub." The brothers in turn tried to blame the murder on Kehoe.

Over the next fortnight, Daniel and James Handley were interrogated on numerous occasions as to their whereabouts on the

Wicklow Courthouse in Market Square and the monument to local 1798 rebellion leader William 'Billy' Byrne who was hanged there in 1799. (photo: NLI)

night of the killing. On the morning of 19 January 1891, police searched Costelloe's farmhouse and found a 17-ounce (almost half a kilo) piece of tobacco and 16 halfpenny coins concealed in the thatch. The tobacco matched the type that was on sale in Mrs. Lyons' shop. The brothers were arrested by Sergeant Gethings of Redcross RIC barracks and on this sparse evidence were charged with the murder of Maryanne Lyons. They were remanded in Wicklow Jail for a week. In an appearance before a magistrate in Redcross police barracks, the older brother Daniel fainted and the inquiry was adjourned. The brothers were finally committed for trial at Rathdrum petty sessions court. Prosecutors decided they should be tried separately.

Daniel Handley appeared in Wicklow Courthouse in August 1891 before Mr. Justice Harrison and a jury. The hearing, which lasted two days, resulted in disagreement among the jury members, who were generally against capital punishment and therefore reluctant to pronounce a guilty verdict. Handley was put on trial for a second time in November in Carlow Courthouse and this again ended in differences among the jurors, unable to agree on a verdict.

Dublin Castle ordered that the trials should be held before a special jury (a device used to exclude Republicans). The brothers were tried on 19 March 1892 before Justice Holmes and a special jury in Wicklow Courthouse. The case was mainly one of circumstantial evidence and based on self-incriminatory statements of the accused. Daniel Handley was found guilty of murder. He had remained calm throughout the proceeding but when sentence of death was about to be passed on him, he screamed "I ain't guilty!" When asked if he had anything to say before sentencing, he shouted: "I didn't strike the final blow!" – perhaps an insight into what happened that night. Both Daniel and James were sentenced to death but the younger brother James, now 17, was believed by the special jury to have been under the influence of his older brother and they recommended mercy.

The verdicts on the young men were very unpopular locally, many believing the Handleys were not the killers. The authorities in Wicklow feared protests in the area if Handley was to be hanged there, but objections were not expected if the punishment was carried out across the border in County Wexford. They were proven correct. However, although there was a chorus of protest in Wexford to the planned hanging in Wexford Jail, the government refused to change the venue.

James's sentence was subsequently commuted to fifteen years penal servitude by the Lord Lieutenant, the Earl of Zetland. In the meantime, the Handleys' parents were forced to move out of Rathnew and they settled in Dublin.

Daniel Handley was moved to Wexford Jail on 21 March 1892 and was to be hanged at 8am on 19 April. The scaffold was erected out of sight in a shed near the prison hospital. The last hanging at the jail was carried out eight years earlier in 1884, when James Tobin was executed for the murder of Eliza Moore. Tobin had killed the elderly woman in Rathdrum, County Wicklow and the motive was also robbery. The hangman was the English executioner, James Berry, and after the hanging was carried out, the inquest that followed in the jail was returned, with a rider added to the effect that "Wicklow prisoners should in future be executed in Dublin."

The hangman in Handley's execution was Thomas Scott, a Yorkshire man and rope-maker by trade. About one hundred people were gathered outside the jail when the prison bell rang out at 7.45am. As Handley was being led towards the shed, Scott quickly placed a white cloth over his head. The prisoner began shaking violently and had to be subdued by prison officers. As the noose was being placed around his neck, he said to the priest who was accompanying him, "Goodbye, Father" to which the priest simply replied, "Goodbye, Dan."

The deputy sheriff of County Wicklow, Edward Davidson, paid the executioner his fee and two hours later the inquest was held in the prison boardroom by Dr. J.R Cardiff, who confirmed the prisoner's death by hanging.

Thomas Scott carried out 17 hangings between 1889 and 1901. From 1892, he was employed as assistant hangman to James Billington, the chief executioner of Great Britain and Ireland. Scott was scheduled to assist Billington in a hanging at Walton Prison in Liverpool on 17 December 1895. Having first reported to the prison on the night before the execution, he picked up a prostitute and they had sex "for about an hour and a half," he claimed. But when he later realized that he had been robbed, he reported the incident to the police. The prostitute later appeared at the police station and his wallet and glasses were recovered and he was prevented from carrying out the planned hanging. Scott was no longer employable in England and so

Wicklow Jail, where the the last man hanged was James Haskins in 1843.

moved to Ireland, where he became chief executioner until 1901. The last hanging he performed was that of John Toole, at Mountjoy Jail in March 1901, after which he lost his job in Ireland when the authorities learned about his past activities in England.

By the late 19th century, the public were calling for fewer hangings and moves were also afoot to reduce the number of prisons in Ireland. Wicklow Jail had closed by 1900 and Wexford Jail in 1903. Wexford Jail became St. Brigid's Centre and was run by the Sisters of St. John of God as a home for intoxicated women. The entrance and perimeter wall survive today but the only original building still standing is the old women's prison block.

The jail functioned as an army barracks from 1921, at the time of the War of Independence. The womens' prison was the scene in 1923 of the executions of Jim Parle, Jack Creane and Pat Hogan during the Civil War. The young anti-Treaty men from Taghmon and Wexford were shot dead by Free State troops, having been arrested for possession of firearms at Horetown House. In 1982, a Garden of Remembrance was opened next to the jail on Hill Street to commemorate the three who were executed.

The prison complex continued to be used as a military barracks until 1931, when it became Wexford County Council headquarters. Wexford District Court was also located here. The county council relocated to its new County Hall headquarters at Carricklawn in 2011. Today the site houses the Centre for Irish Research, in partnership with Georgia Southern University, USA.

Daniel Handley was the last person to be hanged in Wexford Jail. The last execution in Ireland, carried out in Mountjoy Jail, was that of Limerick man Michael Manning in 1954 for the rape and murder of 65-year-old hospital nurse Catherine Cooper. The death penalty was abolished in 1964, except for the murder of gardaí, prison officers and diplomats. In 1990 it was abolished by law for those remaining offences and finally removed from the constitution by a referendum in 2001.

Mining for silver on orders from King Edward VI, aged 12

The ruin of the old silver mine engine house at Barrystown, overlooking Bannow Bay. (photo: Des Kiely)

KING HENRY VIII dispatched a group of experts to Ireland in 1546 in order to ascertain the extent of the country's mineral resources. He proposed that any mines should be worked on behalf on the Crown. But Henry died the next year and was succeeded by his 9-year-old son by Jane Seymour, Edward VI. It was not until 1550 that works began in the Clonmines area of County Wexford on the orders of the new monarch, now aged 12. Because Edward never reached maturity, the realm was governed by a regency council. Known as 'the forgotten Tudor king', he died aged 15 of a lung infection in 1553.

Silver mixed with lead had previously been found in abundance in the locality. The necessary skilled workers were not available in Ireland and so Germans and Cornishmen were brought in to dig the ore from five pits located on the far shore of Bannow Bay opposite Clonmines, at Barrystown. The miners were under the supervision of Bavarian mining expert, Joachim Gundelfinger of Nuremberg and by 1552 a smelting house and stamp mill for crushing the ore were constructed near New Ross.

The Royal Silver Mines at Barrystown were deemed capable of producing 300 ounces of silver per week. A pontoon bridge was built across the Corock

River, presumably at the site of the present-day Wellingtonbridge, to transport the raw ore from Barrystown and stores were established both at Barrystown and Ballyhack. It is recorded that silver ingots, or blocks, were cast in Clonmines for the English Crown. In one tragic incident, the waters of the bay flooded several chambers, killing a number of the miners below ground in the pits. Stories emerged of drunkenness on the site and the mining enterprise fell far short of original expectations. The operational costs of working the mines exceeded their actual yield and so in time the project had to be discontinued.

The site at Barrystown had at least four more documented periods of unprofitable mining activity. In the reign of Elizabeth I, Edward's half-sister, an attempt to revive it was made but yielded little. In 1804-12 the then owner of the land, George Ogle, a retired member for County Wexford in the Irish House of Commons, also endeavoured to make a success of the mine. Brought up in Rossminoge, near Camolin, he wrote the popular 19th century songs *Banna's Banks* and *Moll Ashore*. Ogle lived at Bellevue, Enniscorthy and was a man of wealth but his venture into mining at Barrystown did not make him a profit. A third attempt was made around the year 1840 by the Barrystown Mining Company, established in London. A 31-year lease was signed with the owner of the property, the Rev. Richard King, who was Rector of Mulrankin, at a royalty rent of one-sixteenth part of the ore raised. A high-pressure steam-pumping engine, developed in the early 1800s, now enabled ore deposits to be exploited at much greater depths. *The Wexford Independent* reported in October 1845, around the time of the outbreak of Famine in the country, on the extent of employment at the mines: '*There are at present, employed 16 men on tribute; forty on tut-work; breaking ore on tut-work, ten; surface labourers, six; pitmen, smiths, carpenters, eight; dressers including girls, twelve; buckers, six; boys filling and landing, four – in all from 102 to 120.*' Once again, the Barrystown mines were costing more money to operate than were yielding profit and so they closed in 1849, with many of the labourers and their families taking refuge in the Wexford Workhouse.

The fourth and final endeavour at making the Barrystown mines commercially feasible was made in 1913 by Edward Armstrong Johnson of Ballynapierce House, near Enniscorthy. He was a retired Major General who served in India, Afghanistan and Egypt and then in various departments of the Egyptian Government for 25 years before retiring in 1908. His was the last unsuccessful attempt at reviving the ancient mines. The remains of a Cornish-style engine house and adjoining chimney-stack still stand at the site of what were once the Royal Silver Mines. They lie on private property but within clear view of the main road between Wellingtonbridge and Carrick-on-Bannow.

The town of Clonmines at the head of Bannow Bay. In the foreground the remains of the Augustinian Priory, the tower house on the right is known as the 'Black Castle' and the ruined parish church of St. Nicholas stands behind trees on the left. (photo: Des Kiely)

CLONMINES

One of the best examples of an abandoned medieval town in Ireland, the old port town of Clonmines lies in ruins at the head of Bannow Bay. It was established by the Anglo-Norman knight William Marshal, who also founded the town of New Ross, in the early 13th century. According to Philip Hore's 1901 *History of the Town and County of Wexford*, '*There are few places in Ireland so rich in the ruins of ecclesiastical and defensive buildings of the past. Within the compass of a few acres stand the remains of three churches, portions of monastic buildings, and three castles, those of the Suttons, the Purcells and the FitzHenrys.*'

Today we can see the ruins of the parish church of St. Nicholas with a fortified chapter-house or meeting-house, resembling a tower-house. The Augustinian priory and two tower-houses that were added to the monastery in the 1300s and another two tower-houses dating from the 1400s. There are about 43 surviving fortified tower-houses in County Wexford out of a total of 137, the existence of which have been identified. Also within the remains of the settlement is the gable of a fortified house dating from the early 1600s.

The Augustinian friars came to Clonmines in 1317 to lands given them by the powerful Kavanagh family. The order maintained a strong presence in the area with two further houses in New Ross and one in nearby Grantstown.

The bubonic plague was known as the Black Death because one of the symptoms caused the skin to become black and purple. The disease was carried by fleas on the black rat from Europe, where it killed over 25 million people between 1347 and 1350. It reached the ports of Dublin and Drogheda in 1348, killing more than one-third of the population and probably contributed to the eventual demise of the port town of Clonmines, having spread through County Wexford with intermittent outbreaks continuing into the next century.

St. Nicholas Church is said to have been built for the Augustinian friars in 1385. Records show that the parish church was extended in 1399 by Nicholas FitzNicholas and given the name St. Nicholas. Near the church ruin stands a fortified chapter-house, known as the *Cowboy's Chapel*, which was built around the same time just fifteen feet from the church. Some believe that it had been paid for by a simple cowherd who became massively wealthy and wanted Masses to be offered within for his mother. There is also a cemetery next to the church which is still in use and therefore accessible to the public.

At the height of the Protestant Reformation in Europe, monasteries, often very wealthy and powerful, were dissolved across the continent. Henry VIII was Lord of Ireland and, from 1541, King of Ireland. Friaries accounted for about half of the 400 religious houses in this country. Henry was determined to carry through a policy of dissolution in Ireland and in 1537 introduced legislation into the Irish Parliament. By the time of his death in 1547, around half of the Irish houses had been suppressed. The last abbot of Clonmines was Nicholas Wadding, who surrendered *'a church and belfry, a dormitory, a hall, a kitchen and ceme-*

This map from Hore's 1901 'History of the Town and County of Wexford' shows the head of Bannow Bay with the Owenduff River at the top. The Clonmines ruins are on the left and Barrystown mines on the bottom right.

137

On the right is the ruin of the parish church of St. Nicholas, built in 1385 for the Augustinian friars. On the left is the fortified chapter-house or meeting-house known as the Cowboy's Chapel. (photo: Des Kiely)

tery, and one close within the site thereof' in 1542. The Augustinian priory in Clonmines as well as the Dominican friary in Rosbercon, New Ross, were granted to John Parker, the Master of the Rolls in Ireland. The priory's small parcel of land was divided up and passed through several owners over time. The friars, now homeless, roamed the baronies of Bargy and Forth doing missionary work, visiting the homes of farmers and poor peasants.

In about the year 1735 one of the wandering Augustinian friars, Rev. Nicholas Newport, built a thatched convent and chapel at Grantstown, just two miles from and within view of the old priory at Clonmines. When a later parish church at Kinnagh was demolished there was no church for some time. A small thatched church was built in the graveyard at Ballycullane and as the Penal Laws were relaxed, the building of Catholic churches gathered momentum. The parish church at Ballycullane was replaced in the early 1800s, erected on land donated by Caesar Colclough of Tintern Abbey, who also contributed to its cost. A small community of Augustinian friars resided there until about 1830.

Clonmines was officially given town status in 1574. But over time the river passage gradually silted up, making it difficult to navigate the shallow estuary of mudflats. The silver mines at Barrystown were closed and the houses, church and old priory fell vacant.

In 1684, Robert Leigh of Rosegarland manor near Wellingtonbridge, wrote: *'Clonmines is a very ancient Corporacon, but now quite ruinated, there remaineing onely four or five ruinated Castles, and an old ruined Church called St. Nicholas, and a monastery also ruined which did formerly belong to the order of Augustin, and is called St. Augustins, yet it sends two Burgesses to Parliament still, and was governed by a Portriffe* [magistrate] *and Burgesses* [officials], *but the Charter and contents thereof is worne out of memory long since.'*

Up to the end of the nineteenth century, Clonmines, though lying in ruins, was still classed as a Parliamentary borough, corruptly returning two Members of Parliament to the Irish House of Commons. Regarded as a *rotten borough*, the last 'elected' member of Parliament was Ponsonby Tottenham of Tottenham Green. He also sat for the abandoned town of Bannow and was an uncle of Anne Tottenham of the Loftus Hall poltergeist legend. When the borough was finally disenfranchised in 1800 following the Act of Union and all power was shifted to London, Tottenham was awarded compensation of £487 2s 6d per annum. He subsequently sat in the House of Commons in Westminster as the MP for Wexford Borough between 1801 and 1802, before representing New Ross from 1805 to 1806.

Known as the 'Black Castle', one of the tower houses still standing in Clonmines, was once associated with the FitzHenry and Annesley families. (photo: Des Kiely).

Torpedoed off Hook Head by German U-boats in WWI

A German mine-laying Type UC U-boat during World War I. The 'jumping wire' was stretched between the bow and stern and allowed the submarine to pass under nets and other marine defences. (photo: WikiCommons)

THE GEOLOGICAL Survey of Ireland managed the Irish National Seabed Survey – at the time the world's largest civilian marine mapping programme – between 1999 and 2005. The survey mapped all of Ireland's waters over 200m deep and covering over 600,000 square kilometres. It is estimated that up to 15,000 shipwrecks may lie off Ireland's coast and the survey compiled a database of over 300 of these. Detailed information is contained regarding each wreck's condition on the seafloor, its extent, dimensions and water depth, along with a short background history and the reason for its loss. There is a fascinating Wexford maritime history hidden at the bottom of the sea.

During the First World War (1914-18), Germany employed submarines to lay mines and launch torpedoes against British merchant ships in the Atlantic Ocean in an attempt to stop war-time supplies, such as food and munitions from the United States and Canada. In February 1915, Germany declared a war zone in the waters around Britain and Ireland and U-boat captains were instructed that they could sink merchant ships, even potentially neutral ones, without warning. The British ocean liner RMS *Lusitania*, en route from New York to Liverpool, was sunk on 7 May 1915 by a German U-boat 11 miles off the Old Head of Kinsale, killing 1,198 passengers and crew. Ultimately,

German submarine warfare caused the United States to enter the war after German submarines sank three American merchant vessels on 17 March 1917.

One of the major German shipbuilding companies at the time was A.G. Weber, located on the River Weber in Bremen. The First World War saw the shipyard launch a total of 96 U-boats. During the Second World War, a massive U-boat assembly plant called Valentin was built near Bremen by up to 12,000 forced labourers and concentration-camp inmates. These included 32 Irish seamen, including Patrick Breen from Wexford, who was the first of five to die there. (See separate article 'Nazi concentration camp's slave labourers from Wexford'.) However, the bunker was never completed and not a single one of the revolutionary larger and faster submarines they called the XXI or Elektroboot was ever built by the time the complex was liberated in 1945.

Lying close to the USA-to-Britain shipping route, County Wexford witnessed many attacks by German U-boats on British merchant shipping during World War One. Four of these occurred within a six-month period in 1917 off Hook Head.

SS ANTONY

On St. Patrick's Day 1917, the defensively-armed Antony was one of four vessels sunk over a two-day period off the Wexford and Waterford coasts by U-boat UC-48, which was patrolling the south-east coast. Owned by the Booth

The British merchant ship the SS Antony was sunk south of Hook Head on a journey from Brazil to Liverpool on 17 March 1917 with the loss of 55 lives.

Line of Liverpool, the *Antony* normally carried up to 572 passengers and mail between Britain and South America. On the final leg of its journey from Brazil to Liverpool and carrying a cargo of rubber, four passengers and a crew of 126, the steamship was torpedoed twice, west of the *Coningbeg* lightship anchored off Great Saltee Island. The ship was abandoned immediately but 55 lives were lost and the remaining 75 survivors eventually landed at Queenstown (Cobh). The wreck lies 14km southwest of Hook Head.

SS *KARINA*

The *Karina* was built in Glasgow in 1905 and operated as a passenger liner on the Glasgow and Liverpool service to West Africa. On 30 July 1917, it narrowly escaped being torpedoed during a U-boat attack off the west coast of Ireland. It too was an armed merchant ship and was carrying a 2,000-ton cargo of palm oil and palm kernels from Sierra Leone to Liverpool. Two days later the *Karina*'s captain J.C. Hannay ran out of luck when it was torpedoed off the coast of Hook Head in yet another U-boat attack. As they attempted to evacuate the ship, 4 passengers and 7 crewmen lost their lives. Its sister ship, the SS *Mendi*, was also lost during World War I. It was chartered by the Royal Navy as a troopship and in February 1917, sailing from Cape Town and carrying 823 men to serve in France, a large cargo vessel collided with it in the English Channel.

The SS Karina was torpedoed and sunk in July 1917 with the loss of 11 lives when en route from West Africa to Liverpool.

It sank with the loss of 646 people, most of whom were black South African troops. The wreck of the *Karina*, lying 29 km southwest of Hook Head, was confirmed in 1985 when the ship's bell was recovered.

The Cooroy was sunk off Hook Head after an aborted rescue attempt by a Royal Navy minesweeper.

THE COOROY

A four-masted steel barque built in 1892 in Cumbria and originally named the *Conishead*, the *Cooroy* was one of six four-masted barques known as the 'six sisters'. It was renamed in 1915 when purchased by the London shiping company Scott, Fell & Co. The *Cooroy* was on its final leg of a voyage from Chile to Liverpool on 29 August 1917, carrying sodium nitrate, which was historically mined in Chile and used in the production of fertilizers, pyrotechnics, glass and pottery enamels and food preservatives.

The German mine-laying submarine *UC-75* sighted the ship off Hook Head approaching St. George's Channel when it was attacked with gunfire. The crew of 23, who quickly abandoned the vessel, were rescued by the SS *Glengariff* of the City of Cork Steam Packet Company. They were later landed safely in Queenstown. Hoping to bring the *Cooroy* ashore, seven armed sailors from the minesweeper HMS *Jessamine* boarded the *Cooroy*. But the *UC-75* was still in the area and torpedoed the *Cooroy*, sinking it with the loss of all seven men. In April 1918, HMS *Jessamine* was itself sunk by *U-57* in St. George's Channel with the loss of 41 on board with one survivor.

SS ETAL MANOR

Over a four-day period in September 1917, four ships were sunk by *UC-48* off the Wexford and Waterford coasts. On 19 September, the steamship *Etal Manor* was sailing from Barry in South Wales to Queenstown carrying a cargo of 2,250 tons of coal. About seven miles southwest of Hook Head, it was torpedoed and sunk. The ship's master and five crew were lost. The merchant ship was built just a year earlier in Sunderland for J. Fenwick & Sons of London and was named after Etal Manor House in Northumberland, which at the time was being used as a temporary military hospital for the duration of the war.

U.S. NAVAL AIR STATION WEXFORD

The submarine campaign waged against British and Irish supply lines in the early months of 1917 had become critical. Britain's naval forces were based in Queenstown, which became the centre for anti-submarine forces on the Western approaches. In May 1917, they were joined by United States Navy destroyers, marking the first European presence of the U.S. Navy in World War I. The Royal Navy admiral, Sir Lewis Bayly, was appointed Commander-in-Chief, Coast of Ireland, over the mixed British-American force. The U.S. Navy also set up a network of five Naval Air Stations at Queenstown, Castletownbere, Whiddy Island, Lough Foyle and Wexford.

In early 1918, the U.S. Navy commissioned the seaplane station at Ferrybank, Wexford, to carry out anti-submarine patrols in the area east of Queenstown in an effort to counter U-boat attacks on shipping. The base was quickly erected and incorporated two existing large residences, Ely House and Bann-A-Boo House, which were occupied by naval officers. It was like a small town with its own streets that carried names such as 25th Street, 52nd Street and Broadway. The complex included four large hangars, barracks and even a theatre. It eventually had 20 officers and over 400 men by the end of October 1918. A slipway into the River Slaney was constructed to launch *Curtiss H-16* seaplanes.

The long-range *Curtiss* flying boat was developed in the United

A Curtiss H-16 seaplane, the type used by NAS Wexford.

A Curtiss H-16 seaplane in Wexford Harbour in 1918.

States in response to the challenge in 1913 by the *Daily Mail* newspaper, with a £10,000 prize offered for the first non-stop crossing of the Atlantic by a heavier-than-air aircraft. The *Curtiss* was quickly drafted into wartime use as a patrol and rescue aircraft. The challenge was suspended during the war but renewed in 1919, when the British aviators Alcock and Brown claimed the prize in June 1919. They flew a modified First World War *Vickers Vimy* twin-engined bomber from St. John's, Newfoundland to Clifden, County Galway.

Four *Curtiss H-16* aircraft arrived at Ferrybank on 18 September 1918, eight weeks before the war was to end on 11 November. The seaplanes launched daily from the slipway and bombed several German submarines throughout September and October, making a total of 98 patrol flights.

Wooden barracks at U.S. Naval Air Station Wexford in Ferrybank with hangars in the background and Carcur Bridge seen in the distance.

The station was closed in 1919, with the remaining buildings auctioned and bought by local businesses. The last remaining part of the roof of one of the hangars can be seen above Lily Bloom florists on Custom House Quay. Ferrybank Motors and Ely Hospital now stand on the site of the airbase. Bann-A-Boo House became the Kilcone Lodge Hotel, now the Riverbank House Hotel. The slipway can still be seen today opposite Ferrybank Motors.

Selskar Abbey – site of the first ever Anglo-Irish peace treaty

An engraving of the ruined priory of St. Peter and St. Paul, or Selskar Abbey, published in 1794. The town wall and Selskar Gate, part of the abbey complex, are shown on the extreme left.

A FORCE of about 400 Anglo-Norman knights and archers landed at Bannow Bay in 1169 and were soon joined by an army of 500 under the King of Leinster, Diarmait Mac Murchada. The High King of Ireland, Ruaidrí Ua Conchobair, had overthrown Mac Murchada, who in turn sought the help of King Henry II of England.

The joint force, including the Welsh warrior knight Robert FitzStephen, marched on the Norse-Irish settlement of Waesfjord, later known as Wexford, which was defended by a 2,000-strong army. After two days of fighting and the ships in the harbour burnt on the orders of FitzStephen, the townspeople surrendered to the invaders, having been persuaded to by two bishops. This led to the signing of the first ever Anglo-Irish peace treaty and the swearing of allegiance to Mac Murchada at a ceremony in an earlier church dedicated to the apostles Peter and Paul that stood on the site of Selskar Abbey, overlooking the River Slaney. At the time, long before land reclamation in the 19th century, the river reached what is now Selskar Street. Previously, a Viking temple to the god Odin stood at Selskar – *sel* (seal) *skar* (rock) in Old Norse. These Norsemen, also known as Ostmen in Ireland, may have been responsible for the building of the first church on the site, following their conversion to Christianity around AD 1000.

This newly-constructed temple dedicated to the Norse god Odin was opened on the island of Fyn in Denmark in 2019. It is the first temple to Odin built since the 12th century when the country was Christianized and has been built in the Nordic style with dragon heads. It is thought that a temple to Odin replaced a Christian church that originally stood on the site of Selskar Abbey.

Raymond FitzGerald, nicknamed *le Gros* (the Fat) was one of the commanders of the second phase of the Anglo-Norman invasion, landing at Baginbun in May 1170. Five years later he married Basilia, the only sister of the Earl of Pembroke, Richard de Clare (later known as Strongbow) in the church at Selskar. Strongbow had landed at Passage as part of the second phase.

Strongbow assumed control of Leinster and when Diarmait Mac Murchada died the following year, King Henry II landed in Ireland in October 1171 to assert his position as overlord of the country. He was the first English monarch to set foot in Ireland when he arrived with an army of 4,000 foot soldiers and 500 mounted knights. He allowed Strongbow however to remain Lord of Leinster but retained control of all ports. There is a tradition that Henry spent Lent of 1172 at Selskar, where he did penance for the death of Thomas Becket, the Archbishop of Canterbury. Becket was murdered in 1170 as a result of his defiance of the King's decree that the Church was not above the law of the land.

Robert FitzStephen was promised the control of Wexford town as well as 100,000 acres in the baronies of Forth and Bargy. The lands at Selskar, however, are believed to have been granted to the Roche family, who were of Flemish extraction, and were later responsible for the construction of the tower at Ferrycarrig about 300 years later and Barntown Castle in the 16th century.

An Augustinian priory dedicated to St. Peter and St. Paul was founded by Alexander de la Roche in about 1190 at Selskar. The Anglo-Normans built a stone wall encircling the town in a 'C' shape from West Gate to Castle Gate (next to Wexford Castle on what is now Barrack Street). The priory stood within as well as outside the town wall. However, none of the many monastic buildings that stood beyond the wall survive today. Selskar Gate acted as a connecting gate for the friars and so provided them with toll-free access in and out of the walled town. The nearby West Gate or Cow Gate provided public access to the town on payment of a toll.

From an article on Selskar Abbey in George Griffith's *Chronicles of County Wexford*, published in 1877:

'It was enlarged and endowed by Sir Alexander Roche of Altramont, under singular circumstances. When a young man he became enamoured of a beautiful girl, the daughter of a poor burgess of the town; his parents, to prevent his marriage, prevailed on him to join the crusade then on foot for the recovery of the Holy Sepulchre. On his return from Palestine, he found himself a free agent by their death, but, on revisiting the dwelling of the lady, he ascertained that, in the belief of his rumoured death in battle, the girl had entered a convent. In despair he took a vow of celibacy, and endowed this monastery, dedicating it to the Holy Scripture and became its first prior.'

Selskar was the venue for a Church council, or synod, in 1240, which was convened by the Bishop of Ferns, John of St John. In 1402, King Henry VI granted a licence to the Bishop of Ferns, Patrick Barrett, for the priory to take possession of the church in Ardcavan and in 1418 the chapel of St. Nicholas in Carrig was also granted to the Augustinian priory at Selskar.

When Henry VIII ascended the throne in 1502 he styled himself Lord of Ireland. Pope Clement VII refused his request for an annulment of his marriage to Catherine of Aragon, who had produced no surviving sons. He subsequently broke the Church in England away from the authority of the Pope and the Roman Catholic Church during the English Reformation that transformed England into a Protestant country. Henry appointed himself the Supreme Head of the Church in England and this was confirmed with the passing of the Act of Supremacy in 1534. In that same year, the

This engraving shows how close to the priory the River Slaney flowed, long before land reclamation in the area.

Irish Parliament adopted the Act as well, and the Treasons Act, which resulted in many priests, bishops and lay people who continued to pray for the Pope being imprisoned, tortured and killed. So commenced the dissolution of monasteries, priories, convents and friaries throughout the country.

The priory of St. Peter and St. Paul, Selskar Abbey, was suppressed in 1542 and in 1547 granted to John Parker, secretary to the Lord Deputy of Ireland. Parker, an Englishman and Protestant Reformer, held the office of Constable of Dublin Castle in 1543 and was appointed Master of the Rolls in Ireland in 1552, despite having no apparent legal training. He sat in the Irish House of Commons in 1560. Parker acquired not only Selskar Abbey but also Rosbercon Abbey in Kilkenny on the opposite side of the River Barrow from New Ross, Holmpatrick Abbey near Skerries, Dublin and Tircroghan in Westmeath, making him a very wealthy man.

Some of the priory lands were divided and later fell into the ownership of Philip Devereux, followed by Edward Turner. Selskar subsequently passed to Richard Stafford, who descended from the affluent Kilrane family. In the 15th century, George Stafford built a tower house known as Stafford's Castle, located between Stonebridge and Oyster Lane on South Main Street. The Staffords owned considerable property in Wexford in the 16th and 17th centuries. Richard and his wife Antace, daughter of Leonard Sutton of Ballykeeroge, Campile, were buried in the graveyard at Selskar in 1622.

An extract from an article on Selskar Abbey in the *The Illustrated Dublin Journal*, 1862: 'This church, with six others, were demolished by order of Oliver Cromwell, when in possession of the town in 1649. The churches so destroyed were St. Patrick's [Patrick's Square], St. Mary's [Mary's Lane], St. Bride's [Bride Street], St. John's [John Street], St. Peter's [Peter's Square] and St. Maud's, commonly called Maudlin Town. Not satisfied with levelling these various places of worship, together with the plate belonging to the priory of Selskar, he took possession of a very fine peal of bells, which he shipped for Chester, but which, being of a superior description, were removed a few years afterwards to Liverpool.'

Wexford Castle, located beside Castle Gate, the most southerly gate in the town wall and on high ground overlooking the harbour, was surrendered to Cromwell by its commander, Captain James Stafford. The castle is thought to have been built by King John (1166-1216), youngest son of Henry II. It also

Selskar Church, built in 1826 when the adjacent 500-year-old tower house was restored and converted into a belfry and sacristy. (photo: National Library of Ireland, circa 1900)

functioned as the county jail and was badly damaged by cannon fire from Cromwell's forces during the siege of the town. A military barracks, built on Barrack Street on the site of Wexford Castle, was completed in 1725 and is still standing and in use to this day. Stafford's Castle later became the new jail and continued as such until the new County Jail was built at Westgate in 1812.

The town gates, apart from Selskar Gate, were knocked down in 1759 and, following the rebellion of 1798, replaced by wooden structures that "were so light that children could close them", according to George Bassett's *Wexford County Guide and Directory* (1885). These were finally removed by the Corporation in 1835 on account of being an obstruction to traffic.

The Penal Laws were introduced into Ireland in 1695 and affected eighty percent of the population, who were Catholic, and favoured the minority Church of Ireland. The aim was to eradicate Catholicism from the country. The laws were described by the Irish statesman and philosopher Edmund Burke as "well-fitted for the oppression, impoverishment and degradation of a people as ever proceeded from the perverted ingenuity of man." They were enforced for 134 years until emancipation was finally granted in 1829. Tithes were payable to the Church of Ireland and continued to be demanded up to 1869, when the Church was disestablished under the Church Disestablishment Act.

Selskar Abbey lay in ruin for about 200 years until a Protestant church was proposed to be built on the site in the 1820s. There was huge local opposition, in part because every household in the town was obliged to contribute towards the cost, irrespective of their religion. The plan also involved the demolition of the eastern section of the historic abbey ruins. The person appointed to design Selskar Church was the Irish architect, John Semple (1801-1882). The young architect was taken into partnership by his father, also John Semple, in about 1823. He was also responsible for the design of Monkstown Church in Dublin and St. Mary's Chapel of Ease (known as 'The Black Church') in Broadstone, Dublin. The work included the restoration of the main tower, which was converted into a sacristy and bell tower. The original structure, with its narrow spiral stairway, probably dates to the 1300s. The tower, along with Selskar Gate tower, are the only surviving tower houses in Wexford town. The church was completed in 1826. The building of Selskar Church was followed by the construction of St. Peter's College chapel in the 1830s, the Methodist church on Rowe Street in 1835, Friends' Meeting House in Patrick's

This 1930s postcard depicted the view of Selskar Church and tower from Abbey Street.

Square in 1842 and the Presbyterian church on Anne Street in 1844. The dominant Catholic twin churches on Rowe Street and Bride Street were completed in 1858. They were designed by Wexford architect Richard Pierce, who died four years before they were completed. The decorative railings that surround both churches were manufactured by his younger brother James at his Folly Mills Iron Works, later Pierce's Foundry.

Selskar Church now lies in ruin. Its slate roof fell into disrepair in the 1950s and it was decided to close the church. The belfry tower was renovated again in the 1980s.

Forgotten sinking of the Rosslare-Fishguard ferry in WWII

The SS St. Patrick II, built in 1930 for the Rosslare-Fishguard ferry service. Bombed and sunk near Fishguard in 1941 with the loss of 30 passengers and crew.

THE ROSSLARE to Fishguard ferry *SS St. Patrick II* was registered in Britain and though it flew the Red Ensign, indicating that it was not a military vessel, it was targeted three times by the Luftwaffe in World War Two. It was manned by a mostly Irish crew, and Mosey Brennan from Skeffington Street in Wexford town died from the first attack in 1940. In another assault on Friday 13 June 1941, the ship was sunk with the loss of 17 crew, a gunner and 12 passengers. Many of the dead were Irish and among them was Mosey's son, 17-year-old deckboy John Brennan and Captain Faraday from Arthurstown and his 19-year-old son Jack. But the tragedy has been largely forgotten on this side of the Irish Sea.

Built in Glasgow for the Fishguard & Rosslare Railways & Harbours Company, the *St. Patrick II* went into service on the Fishguard-Rosslare route in 1930. The company was a joint venture between the Great Southern & Western Railway in Ireland and the Great Western Railway in England. The company was responsible for the operation of the ports of Rosslare and Fishguard as well as the ferry service linking them and it also owned the

Waterford to Rosslare railway line, which closed in 2010. When the railways on both sides of the Irish Sea were nationalized, the company came under the joint ownership of British Railways (later British Rail) in 1948 and Córas Iompair Éireann (CIÉ) in 1950.

The *St. Patrick* maintained a vital link during World War II between Rosslare and Fishguard, carrying passengers and mail. It was attacked twice in August 1940 by German warplanes. On the second occasion on 17 August, while heading for Rosslare, about 20 miles off the Wexford coast and in Irish waters, it was hit by machine-gun fire, injuring two on board including crewman Moses (Mosey) Brennan. Mosey (aged 42), who had been shot in the leg, was taken by train from Rosslare to Wexford Station, where he lay in agony on the ground, awaiting transfer to the old Wexford County Hospital. His leg was amputated but he died that night from his injuries.

Just three days after this first attack, the *St. Patrick* was again the target of three German bombers. The vessel was equipped with machine guns, which were immediately deployed and the ship was never hit. It arrived safely in Rosslare, having zig-zagged at full speed to safety. In another incident in November 1940, a mine exploded just 70 yards from the vessel. The passengers and crew were shaken but unhurt and it again returned intact to Rosslare.

Following his death, Mosey's eldest son John, then aged 16, took over as the breadwinner in the family, taking a job after school as a delivery boy

Mosey Brennan from Wexford, who died in Wexford Hospital from his injuries after the St. Patrick was hit by machine-gun fire in 1940.

for Hadden's Medical Hall on Wexford's Main Street. In the autumn of 1940, he announced to his mother that he was going to start a job as a deckhand on the *St. Patrick* in order to earn more money for the family.

Shortly after midnight on Friday 13 June 1941, the *St. Patrick* left Rosslare in calm water on its regular sailing to Fishguard, carrying 44 passengers and 45 crew. Four hours later at 4.20am, when the ship was eleven miles out from Strumble Head Lighthouse on the Welsh coast, an alarm was sounded. Stewardess Elizabeth May Owen, a 40-year-old Fishguard native, along with fellow stewardess Jane Hughes, began running around helping passengers, most of whom had been asleep on the lower deck, to get their lifebelts on and move to the upper deck. A Luftwaffe dive-bomber had circled above the vessel and now returned, dropping a 'stick' of four bombs. They went straight through the bridge and set the ship's oil tanks on fire, resulting in the vessel splitting in two. All the senior crew on the bridge, including the ships's master, Captain James Faraday, were killed. Stewardess Jane Hughes also perished.

Captain James Faraday, originally from Arthurstown, along with his son Jack, perished on board the St. Patrick when it sank in 1941.

Sixty-three-year-old Faraday was born in Arthurstown in 1878 and lived in Goodwick, near Fishguard. His son Jack, a 19-year-old merchant navy cadet, who was home on leave, had travelled with his father on the *St. Patrick* simply for a day trip. Jack, who was a strong swimmer and could easily have saved himself, swam back to the sinking ship in a desperate attempt to save his father. But Captain Faraday was already dead, having been killed in the initial bomb blasts, and Jack tragically drowned. A nephew of Captain Faraday, Joe Wallace from Duncannon, survived the sinking.

Two able seamen, John Kent from Duncannon and another Wexfordman by the name of Kennedy, managed to launch one of the lifeboats and got the surviving passengers on board. Seven minutes after being hit, the *St. Patrick* slipped beneath the waves. The survivors were later picked up by Royal Navy patrol ships and landed at Milford Haven, where they were treated in hospital.

From *The Times* newspaper on 17 June 1941: 'Nicholas Rossiter, a passenger, said: "We were asleep below when we heard a terrific crash. I rushed on deck and saw that the boat was listing badly. I immediately jumped into the sea and got hold of a raft. Here I was joined by two women, one of whom was badly injured. It was blowing hard, and our raft was carried about by the sea and at times almost capsized. After about an hour we were picked up by a warship."

Thirty people lost their lives and among the Irish fatalities was the young Wexford deckboy John Brennan, then aged 17. One of the passengers who died was Thomas Murray from Macroom, Co. Cork, a British Army soldier on his way back to his regiment in England. He was an uncle of RTÉ's Charlie Bird. The ship's ticket collector, 60-year-old Edmund Roche from Mallow, Co. Cork also perished.

Mosey Brennan's daughter Alice was 10 when she lost her father and eldest brother. Her mother had to raise the family on a British war-widow's pension and Alice later moved to Birmingham, where she married Norman Hunt, a member of the Coldstream Guards, in 1952. Over forty years later, in 1994, the couple settled in Mulgannon in Wexford. Alice has spent years fighting for recognition from the Irish government for the Irish passengers and crew who lost their lives on board the *St. Patrick*. Her father and brother had never been recognized by the State and the official line was that "because the ship flew a British flag, it was up to Britain to recognize those killed."

The story was taken up by Wexford writer and broadcaster Shane Dunphy, who produced *'The Sinking of the Saint Patrick'* for RTÉ Radio's *Doc on One* series in 2012. This finally led a number of months later to the unveiling at Rosslare Europort of a plaque recognizing the sacrifice that people on board the ill-fated vessel made — seventy years after the tragedy. As well as Alice and her husband in attendance as guests of honour, Beryl Kinsella was there to remember her father Arthur Walters who survived the attack. He was saved by a British destroyer that picked him up from a wooden raft.

Elizabeth May Owen, ship's stewardess, was the daughter of Fishguard

Elizabeth May Owen with fellow St. Patrick crew members, Norman Campbell (chief radio officer) and Francis Purcell (second engineer) after they were awarded Lloyd's Medals at a ceremony in London in 1941.

dock porter William Thomas Owen. She became the first woman to receive both the Lloyd's Medal for 'bravery at sea' and the George Medal for her 'act of great bravery' in saving passengers trapped in the lower deck. The WWII heroine's grave was finally rediscovered by historians in a quiet corner of a Strumble Head cemetery near Fishguard in 2017. Elizabeth May had been employed on the ferries out of Fishguard for most of her working life and died in 1972 at the age of 71.

Following the sinking of the *St. Patrick II*, the service between Rosslare and Fishguard was suspended for the duration of the war. Its sister ship the *St. David* was also bombed and sank with the loss of 57, including its captain, in 1944. The *St. David*, clearly marked as a hospital ship, was returning from the Anzio landings in Italy with wounded Allied troops when it was deliberately sunk by German aircraft.

Shortly after the sinking of the *St. Patrick II*, the ship's masthead pennant was washed ashore at Fishguard. The flag was transferred to its replacement vessel, the *St. Patrick III*, which was launched in 1948.

The British-registered *St. Patrick*, named after the patron saint and carrying so many Irish passengers and crew, is hardly remembered in Ireland despite having lost many Irish people including Captain James Faraday from Arthurstown, along with his son Jack, and Mosey Brennan and his son John from Wexford.

After 70 years, this plaque was unveiled at Rosslare Europort in 2012 to finally recognize the victims of the sinking of the St. Patrick back in 1941.

THE SS IRISH PINE

(sunk in 1942, no survivors)

This steam merchant ship was built in Seattle in 1919 and named *West Hematite*. It was chartered by Irish Shipping Ltd. in Dublin from the US Shipping Board for the duration of the Second World War and renamed *Irish Pine*. It was clearly painted with 'EIRE' on its sides, indicating its neutrality.

On 16 Nov 1942, en route from Dublin to Boston and unescorted, the *Irish Pine* was chased for eight hours by German U-boat, *U-608*, in rough

The Irish Pine, with clear markings indicating its neutrality during WWII.

weather and stormy seas with rain and snow squalls. Apparently its neutrality markings were not spotted in the poor visibility. Positioned south of Newfoundland, the *Irish Pine* was hit in the stern by a single torpedo from a distance of 800 metres and sank in just 3 minutes. The crew was observed abandoning ship by the U-boat sailors and starting to take to a lifeboat but the Germans did not offer assistance and all on board perished.

The crew of 33 were all Irish, four of them from Wexford. They were: Captain Matthew O'Neill, Patrick Bent (carpenter), Patrick Cleary (engineer) and Stephen Smith (boatswain). *U-608* was itself sunk two years later in the Bay of Biscay by the British Navy and RAF aircraft but all 52 crewmen survived.

THE CYMRIC
(vanished in 1944, no survivors)
The *Cymric* was an old iron schooner built in North Wales in 1893. It was sold to Captain Richard Hall of Arklow in 1906 and was engaged in the Spanish wine trade and also worked the South America route. During the First World War, the *Cymric* served as an armed British decoy vessel, attempting to lure U-boats into range and then opening fire, but it had little success.

After the war, it was disarmed and returned to Arklow and for the next twenty years transported malt from Cork, New Ross and Wexford to Dublin. In a memorable incident in 1921, the *Cymric* collided with a tram in Ringsend in Dublin. While waiting for a bridge to open, it was caught by a gust of wind and blown towards the bridge, a wooden boom pierced the tram but nobody was injured.

In 1922, the *Cymric* struck the Brandy Rocks, south of the Saltee Islands, and had to be beached. In another incident on Christmas Eve 1933, it struck a bank in Wexford Harbour and spent five days there before eventually being refloated, after some barrels of malt were removed from its cargo.

On 23 February 1944, under the command of Captain Christopher Cassidy from Athboy Co. Meath, the *Cymric* left Ardrossan in Scotland, bound for Lisbon with a cargo of coal. The last sighting of the ship was the following day as it passed close to Dublin Bay. It was never seen again. Perhaps it hit a mine, was sunk by a U-boat or blown off course into a prohibited shipping area and sunk by Allied aircraft or warships.

The crew of 11 were never seen again and 6 of them were Wexford men: Kevin Furlong (engineer), Michael Tierney (engineer), Philip Bergin, James Brennan, James Crosbie and William O'Rourke.

Not far from where the *Cymric* collided with the tram, a new residential street off Seán Moore Road was named Cymric Road in the newly developed Dublin Docklands.

The schooner Cymric, on what was to be its last voyage and with a mostly Wexford crew, vanished with all hands en route to Lisbon in 1944.

Providing shelter for Wexford's poor and destitute

Wexford Workhouse opened in 1845, it later operated as Wexford County Hospital from 1928 to 1992 and now lies derelict. (photo: Des Kiely)

THE FIRST Irish 'house of industry' was established in 1703 in Dublin 'for the employment and maintaining the poor thereof'. It was constructed on the site of the present-day St. James's Hospital and by 1771 there was one in every county. In 1838, the Irish Poor Law Act was passed to create a system of relief for the persistent poverty that plagued the country. A total of 130 Poor Law Unions were created on the island, all funded by a poor rate – a relief tax that was levied on property in each parish. Only ratepayers were eligible to be elected annually to the Boards of Guardians, thereby largely excluding native Irish, most of whom were tenants at this time.

Architect George Wilkinson designed all 130 workhouses in Ireland, built between 1839 and 1842.

English architect George Wilkinson won a workhouse design competition in 1835 and, having designed many in England, he was invited to Ireland in 1839 as the architect of the Poor Law Commission. He designed all 130 workhouses following the commission's brief that 'the style of building is intended to be of the cheapest description compatible with durability...all mere decoration being studiously excluded.' All workhouses were completed by 1842. Wilkinson later designed a number of train stations in the country, including Harcourt Street Railway Station in 1858 for the Dublin Wicklow and Wexford Railway Company.

In 1840, four Poor Law Unions were formed in County Wexford. Workhouses were completed two years later at Enniscorthy (now St. John's Hospital), New Ross (replaced with the Fever Hospital and now the New Houghton Hospital) and Gorey (the site is now occupied by Gorey Business Park). The workhouse in Wexford (now derelict) was built on the site of 'Somerton', the former residence of John Redmond (great-grandfather of the politician of the same name, who became leader of the Irish Parliamentary Party in 1900). However, due to difficulties collecting the poor rate, the three-storey Wexford Workhouse was delayed, finally declared fit for admissions three years later in 1845.

It was estimated at the time that 2.3 million people in Ireland were living on the verge of starvation. The workhouse, also known as the poorhouse, was intended as a place of refuge for the most poverty-stricken and destitute. Over time, this was extended to include the aged and infirm, abandoned babies and children, orphans and mentally ill poor. Although entry into a workhouse was voluntary, it was also a place of punishment for vagabonds and 'disorderly' women. Conditions were miserable for the inmates. Rules and regulations were harsh in order to discourage able-bodied people from entering to avail of free food and accommodation.

When a family entered, they were segregated and put into separate male, female and children's units and communication between them was forbidden. Male and female accommodation wings were located on either side of the complex. There were separate schoolrooms for boys and girls, with the children's dormitories

Children over seven were separated from their parents on arrival in the workhouse.

above. Dormitories were cramped and beds consisted of wooden planks and a straw mattress covered in rags. The wards lacked ventilation and toilet facilities were large, often overflowing, urination tubs.

New arrivals suffering from any infectious illness were placed in the infirmary block behind the workhouse that also contained wards for 'idiots'. Bathing regulations stated: 'Every patient to be bathed immediately after

Men, women and children ate separately in the workhouse dining-room.

admission, and once a week afterwards, unless exempted by medical order'. A standard-issue uniform made of a hard-wearing, coarse material was issued to all arrivals. Their own clothes were washed and disinfected and stored, along with any other possessions, in the attic rooms.

Workhouse conditions were never to be better than those enjoyed by the population outside, whose diet was often barely above subsistence level. After roll call at 6.30am, breakfast consisted of stirabout (oatmeal porridge) with buttermilk. Dinner comprised either potatoes and buttermilk only, or with a meat-soup twice weekly. Another option for the workhouse was to add a supper of oatmeal porridge with buttermilk and bread but no meat-soup for dinner. Bedtime was 8pm.

In return for their upkeep, those able to were forced to work at least eleven hours a day. The women were mostly engaged in domestic work such as cooking, cleaning, laundry and sewing. The men worked at building, carpentry or farming. Stone-breaking was another task often given to male inmates. It was physically demanding and the results were sold for road-mending. Inmates were not allowed out without permission. Punishments for those who broke the rules included no dinner for a week, a lashing or solitary confinement.

THE GREAT FAMINE

The disease known as 'blight' that attacks the potato crop is believed to have originated in either Mexico or South America and spread to North America. In 1843-44, the potato harvest was largely destroyed around the ports of New York and Philadelphia. It was transported across the Atlantic with a shipment of seed potatoes for Belgian farmers and by mid-August 1845 northern France, The Netherlands and southern England were affected. In September 1845, two months after the Wexford Workhouse opened its doors, *The Gardeners' Chronicle* announced: 'We stop the press with very great regret to announce that the potato murrain [blight] has unequivocally declared itself in Ireland.'

This plaque in Ballygarrett church grounds commemorates the first notification of potato blight in Ireland in August 1845.

Potato blight in the country was first detected in County Waterford and in Killegney near Clonroche, County Wexford in August 1845, though this county would not be as badly affected as others. A memorial plaque in Ballygarrett church grounds bears the inscription: *'The potato blight/ phytophthora infestans which was the Great Irish Famine of 1845-49 was first detected on 18 August 1845 at Killegney, Clonroche, Co. Wexford. A similar outbreak was noticed at Oldtown near Ferns on the following day'*. Many of the potatoes in the ground were found to have gone black and rotten and their leaves had withered. In late August, the blight was observed at the Botanical Gardens in Dublin but this was initially not made public. On 6 September 1845, both the *Dublin Evening Post* and the *Waterford Freeman* grimly reported that the spread of the blight was already considerable and warned of the likelihood of famine.

A third of the potato crop was wiped out that year. But Wexford was a relatively prosperous farming region with a higher than average emphasis on tillage farming for grain crops. Much of the rest of the country lacked industrial development but malting, iron foundries and the maritime trade saved Wexford from the worst ravages of the period.

The Corn Law of 1784 restricted the import of grain from Britain into Ireland in order to protect Irish growers. But with the onset of the Famine the landlords of Leinster, many of whom cultivated grain, continued to still sell to the large markets in Britain. Robert Peel's Tory government in Westminster, however, repealed the Corn Laws in 1845 and arranged for maize to be imported into Ireland from Britain and the USA. This was distributed at cost price by a Relief Commission. The government also set up a Board of Works that initiated road-building schemes to keep unemployment down.

But in 1847, the Whigs, under John Russell, gained power. Some merchants in Ireland were complaining about the cheap imports. The Whig government limited aid to the Irish famine and held an evangelical belief that 'the judgement of God sent the calamity to teach the Irish a lesson'. The financial onus for famine relief was now legally on Irish landlords, who in turn tried to save money by ejecting tenants from their properties. Tenants were forced to clear the land of what was often their crudely built mud cabin before gaining access to the workhouse. Some landlords paid towards their fares to emigrate.

Under the Board of Works schemes a semi-starved population was compelled to toil for ten hours a day. They built walls, dug drainage ditches and broke rocks for the construction of roads, bridges and harbours for a paltry relief wage to buy food. A large part of the population depended on this money and therefore had no choice but to accept the cruel conditions in order to put food on the table. In Wexford, land reclamation works began with the building of the North Slob embankment and the Cull Bank at Ballyteige Lough.

The potato harvest of 1847 was successful but by then too many people had moved off the land and into Public Works schemes. Not enough potatoes had been planted that spring and so there was still a food shortage. In what became known as Black '47, the number of deaths from disease rather than starvation increased and a quarter of a million people emigrated.

The old Wexford Workhouse complex now lies abandoned. (photo: Ireland from the Skies)

When more than £4 million had been paid out in wages, it was decided to scrap the Public Works schemes in March 1847. Under a new Destitute Poor Act, soup kitchens were set up in all Poor Law Union areas of the country and by August meagre rations were being given to three million people across the country.

By July 1849, 200,000 people were living in workhouses, with 800,000 receiving relief outside. Throughout the Famine, the workhouses never managed to keep up with demand, so overcrowding was always present. The capacity of Wexford Workhouse was 600 but the number of occupants increased almost threefold, peaking at 1,771 during the Famine. The Gorey workhouse, built for 500 people, had 975 inmates by 1848. Enniscorthy was built to accommodate 600 and New Ross 900 but these numbers swelled too. Fever, malnourishment and disease were rife in the workhouses. In the first four months of 1848, 188 people, including 41 infants, died in the Wexford Workhouse. Malnourishment and tuberculosis were the two main causes of adult deaths. In 1848, men were sent from the workhouse into Wexford town to disinfect the streets in order to try to curtail the spread of cholera.

Many entered the workhouses to assure themselves of a coffin and burial at public expense. Most ended up in mass graves in the Paupers' Graveyard, located off Coolcott's Lane. They got no obituary, proper funeral or headstone. Some family members simply placed a stone to mark the resting place of their loved ones. Children suffered particularly badly in the workhouses, with forty per cent of those who remained being either orphaned or deserted. The population of County Wexford fell by about twenty per cent, mostly through emigration. By the end of the Famine far more people had died from diseases such as dysentry and scurvy as well as cholera than direct starvation.

The Paupers' Graveyard off Coolcott's Lane in Wexford town. The inscription on the headstone reads: 'In this place, known only to God, lie the bodies of Wexford's poor, deprived, handicapped and destitute. Remember them'.
(photo: Des Kiely)

Young Enniscorthy man's body never found in 1916 shelling

Thomas Wafer was shot in Dublin during the 1916 Rising and his body was never recovered, having been burnt after shelling by a British warship.

THOMAS WAFER was shot and killed by a sniper's bullet on 26 April 1916, while he occupied the Hibernian Bank on the corner of Sackville Street and Lower Abbey Street during the Easter Rising in Dublin. The building and much of Lower Abbey Street was later shelled by the Royal Navy warship RMS *Helga*, which was positioned on the River Liffey, below Butt Bridge. Buildings in the area were engulfed by fire and reduced to shells and piles of rubble. The 26-year-old's body was never recovered.

Thomas was the eldest child of Patrick and Dorah (née Keegan) Wafer and was born in Enniscorthy in 1890. His father was employed as a clerk in a flour store and the family lived in the Templeshannon area of the town, close to historic Vinegar Hill. The family name is often misspelt 'Weafer' but the census return of 1901 verifies the correct spelling.

The signature of Thomas's father Patrick Wafer as it appears on the 1901 census return.

Aged 21, Thomas was living and working in Galway as a cabinet-maker. He was one of six boarders in the home of sisters Delia and Margaret Hanley in High Street, both shopkeepers and daughters of farmer Michael Hanley. In 1912, Thomas married Margaret in Dublin and their daughter Mary was born the following year. They lived on the city's northside, where Thomas had his own upholstery and cabinet-making shop.

He joined the Irish Volunteers and rose quickly through the ranks, serving as Captain of 'E' Company in the 2nd Dublin Battalion in the aftermath of the Howth gun-running incident in July 1914. Nine hundred rifles from Hamburg were landed on the *Asgard* – a yacht owned by Erskine Childers. Along with his brother Paddy, who worked for Lipton's Tea Company on North Wall, Thomas was involved in procuring arms in the run-up to the Rising and they distributed them from Thomas's flat on North Circular Road. In

Paddy Wafer, younger brother of Thomas, also fought in the Rising in Dublin. He was sentenced to six months hard labour in Stafford Jail and was later interned in Frangoch internment camp in Wales.

August 1915, Thomas was in charge of a raid by a party of six, which included his brother Paddy, on the London & North Western railway depot at North Wall. Over a hundred rifles and explosives were seized. The arms had been legally imported and were intended for John Redmond's National Volunteers.

A group within the Irish Volunteers, along with IRB members led by Pádraig Pearse, had secret plans to launch an armed rebellion on Easter Sunday 1916. But on hearing of the failed attempt by Roger Casement to import arms on Good Friday, the chief-of-staff Eoin O'Neill cancelled all activity by placing a last-minute advertisement in the *Sunday Independent*. This led to great confusion around the country.

On Easter Monday, 24 April, Thomas mobilized his men in Fairview and posted a unit to nearby Ballybough Bridge to confront a contingent of British troops who were advancing into the city from Dollymount. He then went to see James Connolly, who gave orders that his battalion was to make their way immediately to Sackville Street to take part in the Rising. Wafer rounded up around 100 Volunteers in the Fairview and Summerhill area and they marched to the GPO, arriving around 3pm. They were sent across the street to occupy the block of buildings stretching from Lower Abbey Street to Eden Quay. They were to make the Hibernian Bank building on the corner of Sackville Street and Lower Abbey Street their headquarters. Members of Cumann na mBan, the republican women's paramilitary organization, were to cook meals and nurse any Volunteers who may get injured in the fighting.

On the opposite corner stood Reis's Jewellers, which housed the Dublin Wireless School of Telegraphy on its upper floors. From here that evening the Proclamation was broadcast to the outside world in morse code: "Irish Republic declared in Dublin today. Irish troops have captured city and are in full possession. Enemy cannot move in city. The whole country rising."

On Tuesday afternoon, Thomas was wounded and received treatment in the GPO from Dr. J.J. Tuohy and members of Cumann na mBan. The next day, 26 April, he returned to his post in the Hibernian Bank. While walking upstairs he was shot in the stomach through a landing window. The shot came from a sniper on the roof of McBirney's department store on Aston Quay. Before dying, he was attended by nurse Leslie Price, a member of Cumann na mBan, who had just time to say a prayer in Wafer's ear. He was believed to have been shot by Private Alfred Tyler of the Sherwood Foresters, who in turn died from a gunshot wound to the head three days later. Richard Corbally, a member of the Irish Citizen Army, is credited with killing Tyler.

The remaining shell of the Hibernian Bank on Sackville Street at the corner Lower Abbey Street, Dublin in the aftermath of shelling by the British warship RMS Helga in 1916.

The continuous broadcasts from Reis's building were intercepted by both the wireless operator on board HMS *Adventure,* moored in Kingstown Harbour, and the listening station at Caernarvon in Wales. As fighting continued in the city the next day, artillery in the grounds of Trinity College and on the British gunboat HMS *Helga* began firing on Volunteer positions. Liberty Hall and much of the Sackville Street area was shelled from a position behind Butt Bridge and the Loopline railway bridge over the Liffey. Reis's and the entire block as well as the Hibernian Bank building were hit and burnt to the ground. Soon the GPO and many buildings on Sackville Street and nearby streets were in flames. Thomas Wafer's body was lost in the fire and was never recovered.

> When the *Helga* steamed up the Liffey from its moorings in nearby Kingstown, the end was in sight for the Easter Rising in central Dublin. Ironically, the *Helga* was built in Liffey Dockyard in 1908 for the Department of Agriculture, and its principal function was fishery protection. When World War I broke out, the ship was pressed into service as an anti-submarine patrol vessel in 1915. The *Helga* was one of the first ships to the scene of the sinking RMS *Leinster,* torpedoed about 16 miles out from Kingstown in 1918. It managed to save over 90 passengers but in total 600 people lost their lives. The *Helga* was acquired by the Irish Free State in 1923 and renamed *Muirchú* ('hound of the sea'), becoming one of the first ships in the Irish Navy. The following year, the *Muirchú* resumed life as a fishery patrol vessel, now flying the Irish flag. In 1947 the *Muirchú* was sold for scrap but while on its final journey to Dublin to be scrapped, it sank off the Saltee Islands without loss of life. The ship's wheel was salvaged by local divers and was at one time on display in Kehoe's Bar in Kilmore Quay.

Part of a letter written by Thomas Wafer *(right)* a few hours before he was killed include the words "...all will be quiet in a few hours don't worry..." The letter fragment was verified by his sister in 1953 and is included in the 'Letters 1916' digital archive begun in 2013 by Maynooth University. The collection includes thousands of letters that make reference to the Easter Rising.

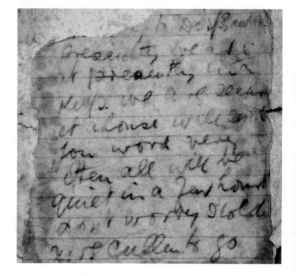

Thomas left behind his wife Margaret and their two-year-old daughter Mary Eliza. They went to live with Margaret's brother, a farm labourer, in Tuam, Co. Galway. In 1923, Margaret wrote the following letter to Richard Mulcahy, then Chief-of-Staff of the National Army:

General Mulcahy

GHQ, Portobello Barracks, Dublin

Dear General

As I the widow of Thomas Joseph Wafer Capt. E Company 2nd Battalion killed in action in Dublin April 26th 1916 would like to lay my case before you as I have one girl 9½ years and since then I had to come and live with my brother. I am in a bad way ever since then and I would feel very grateful to you if you would do your best for me. I know you have done so for me and my equals as since I have lost him I was left on my own to do the best I could for myself. Well I know it doesn't require to be written about but I was advised to let you know my position for the past seven years depending on my brother. If you require any further particulars I will be only too pleased to send it on.

Yours faithfully

Mrs Wafer

Richard Mulcahy married Min Ryan in 1919. The Ryans from Tomcoole, Taghmon, Co. Wexford, were a well-known republican family. Min was a founding member of Cumann na mBan in 1914. She served in the GPO during the Rising along with her sister Phyllis and brother James, who later became TD for Wexford, serving from 1918 to 1965. Mulcahy took part in the fighting in Ashbourne in County Meath on

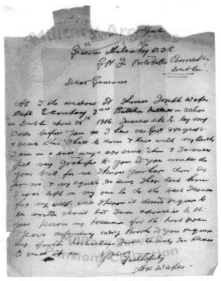

Letter written by Margaret Wafer to General Richard Mulcahy, seeking financial help for herself and her daughter. (Irish Military Archives)

Easter Monday, one of the few military actions of the 1916 Rising to take place outside Dublin. He was a supporter of the Anglo-Irish Treaty of 1921 and succeeded Michael Collins as Commander-in-Chief of the National Army. He was a founding member of the Cumann na nGaedheal party and was later leader of the Fine Gael party.

On Holy Thursday 1916, Min Ryan delivered a dispatch from Seán McDermott to the Volunteers in Enniscorthy with word that the Rising was going to take place on Easter Sunday. However, she was back again on Saturday delivering Eoin McNeill's countermanding order. Patrick Wafer, the father of Thomas and Paddy, took part in the Enniscorthy Rising, which lasted four days and was led by Wexford journalist Robert Brennan. Patrick joined the Volunteers in 1913 and was a member of the IRB. Before the Rising he was involved in collecting gold to purchase arms at the request of Thomas Clarke. Nobody died in the Enniscorthy Rising and the insurgents surrendered to retired British Army Officer, Colonel George French of Newbay House, Wexford on 1 May on the instructions of Pádraig Pearse, from his prison cell in Arbour Hill. Pearse had been unaware of the activity in Enniscorthy.

Thomas and Paddy's mother Dorah died in 1929, aged 58. Their father Patrick remarried and he died aged 74 in 1944. Thomas and Margaret's daughter Mary married a Galway hairdresser in 1931 and they settled in the city. In 1944, Margaret, the widow of Thomas, died aged 62, in Dublin.

Two plaques in Irish and English dedicated to the memory of Captain Thomas Wafer were erected by the National Graves Association on the 20th anniversary of the Rising in 1936. They were fixed to the exterior of the rebuilt Hibernian Bank building on Sackville Street, renamed O'Connell Street in 1924, which today houses a branch of Permanent TSB Bank.

New Street in Enniscorthy was renamed Weafer Street after Thomas Wafer. The misspelt name was corrected and the street renamed in the centenary year of 2016. Thomas Wafer Memorial Hall in Spring Valley, Enniscorthy was also re-dedicated. Moira Riddick, granddaughter of Captain Wafer, was present at the renamings.

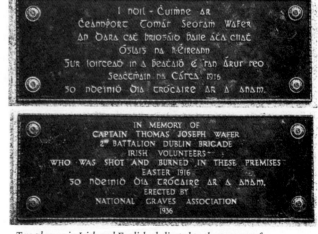

Two plaques in Irish and English, dedicated to the memory of Captain Thomas Wafer. They were erected on the building that now houses a branch of Permanent TSB Bank on the corner of O'Connell Street and Lower Abbey Street, by the National Graves Association in 1936, the 20th anniversary of the Rising.

Wexford baker was hanged, drawn and quartered

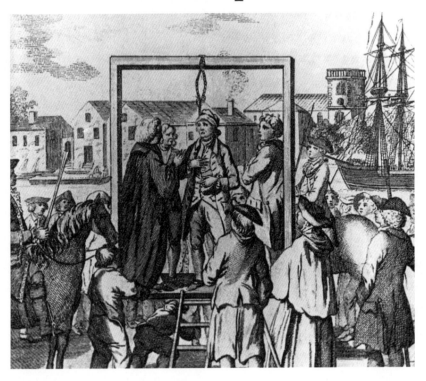

MATTHEW LAMBERT, along with five other Catholics, was hanged, drawn and quartered in the centre of Wexford town in 1581. 'The Wexford Martyrs' were found guilty of aiding Viscount Baltinglass, James Eustace, and a Jesuit priest to escape from Ireland. They had also been found guilty of refusing to take the Oath of Supremacy, which declared Elizabeth I head of the Church.

The House of Tudor, under King Henry VIII, introduced Protestantism as the state religion in England in 1534. The English monarch was to be 'the only supreme head on earth of the Church in England' in place of the Pope. Allegiance to the Church in Rome was now considered treasonous. This led to the dissolution of monasteries and in Wexford town the properties of Selskar Abbey and the Franciscan Friary were confiscated. They were granted to tenants loyal to the Crown and the new Protestant religion.

Religious persecution was inaugurated in Ireland and in 1536, Henry VIII appointed George Browne as Protestant Archbishop of Dublin and Primate of Ireland. According to the 17th century *Annals of the Kingdom of Ireland*, friars and monks throughout the land were massacred, having refused to acknowledge the spiritual supremacy of the King. Browne became the King's main instrument to enforce the new religion in the country. The Archbishop and some members of his Council set out on a 'visitation' to counties Wexford, Carlow, Waterford and Tipperary. The *Annals* recorded an account from their expedition on 18 January 1539: "The day following we kept the sessions there [at Wexford]. There was put to execution four felons, accompanied with another, a friar, whom we commanded to be hanged in his habit, and so to remain upon the gallows for a mirror to all his brethren to live truly."

Elizabeth I, Queen of England and Ireland, tried to impose Protestantism on the Irish people throughout her reign from 1558 to 1603.

Henry was succeeded in 1553 by his daughter Mary Tudor, who was raised Catholic. Queen Mary attempted to purge Protestantism from the country and reverse the English Reformation. Her father's Act of Supremacy was repealed in 1554 and Catholicism was reinstituted as England's state religion. Mary had over 280 religious dissenters burned at the stake, earning her the name 'Bloody Mary'.

Queen Mary was succeeded in 1558 by her younger half-sister Elizabeth I as queen. One of her first actions was the re-establishment of the Protestant Church. A new Act of Supremacy declared the Church of England's independence from Rome and Elizabeth was given the title of Supreme Governor by parliament. Although Ireland was not formally a realm, Elizabeth assumed the title Queen of Ireland, as had her sister Mary before her. Anglicanism was imposed as the state religion in the country, as well as English law, language and culture.

Ireland was divided between the mainly Gaelic-speaking Irish and the 'Old English' (those of Norman-Irish extraction), who lived in the English Pale.

This area included Dublin, Kildare, Meath and Louth and stretched from Dundalk to Dalkey. The Pale was directly under the control of the English government and its boundary was fortified by earthen banks and trenches. The baronies of Forth and Bargy, which survived undisturbed from the time of the Anglo-Norman invasion, were later regarded as the Wexford Pale. 'Beyond the pale' meant you were outside the authority and safety of English law, and subject to all the 'savageries' of rural Ireland.

Queen Elizabeth feared that her arch enemy King Philip II, the Catholic king of Spain, would send forces to Ireland and from there attack England. She therefore needed Ireland to be loyal to her. Philip had married her sister Mary Tudor in 1554. A devout Catholic, the King saw himself as a defender of Catholic Europe against the Protestant Reformation. In 1588, he decided to invade England directly from La Coruña in Galicia, sending a fleet of 130 ships to overthrow Elizabeth and her Protestantism in England. But English warships attacked the Spanish armada off the south coast of England and they were chased up the east coast. The larger, multi-decked Spanish galleons were forced to sail round the north of Scotland and then southwards off the west coast of Ireland. But they were hit by violent storms and about 24 were wrecked along the rocky coast from Antrim to Kerry, with the loss of about 6,000 lives. Many of the survivors were put to death by hanging, on the instructions of the Lord Deputy, William FitzWilliam in Dublin.

Religious persecution of Catholics continued in Ireland, though Elizabeth also feared that the crackdown might drive those Catholic defenders into the hands of Gaelic rebels. At first she treated Gaelic chiefs as good subjects but the English military in Ireland preferred to use force to crush opposition. Elizabeth personally expressed a desire to learn Gaelic and demanded the translation of the New Testament and insisted that the vernacular be used in church services. A phrase book in Irish, Latin and English was compiled by the Earl of Westmeath, Sir Christopher Nugent, for Elizabeth

Extract from an Irish, Latin, English phrase book compiled by the Earl of Westmeath for Elizabeth I.

but the New Testament was not translated until after her death.

English, Scottish and Welsh were granted lands held by Gaelic clans and Hiberno-Norman families in Ulster, Munster, parts of the midlands and North Wexford to 'civilize the natives'. The Ulster counties were planted with mainly Protestant Scottish settlers. Many of the colonists also engaged in land grabs, having led the natives into hopeless rebellions. One such planter was Sir Walter Raleigh, who was granted 42,000 acres in Youghal and Lismore as part of the Munster Plantation. Raleigh is said to have introduced tobacco from Virginia for the first time into England in 1586.

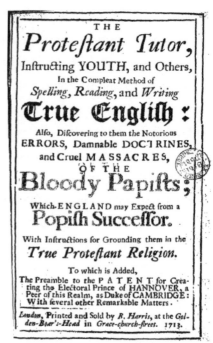

The Protestant Tutor, an anti-Catholic book by Benjamin Harris, first published in 1681.

When Queen Elizabeth was tempted to try smoking in 1600, the habit was copied by much of the population and soon became commonplace.

Violence and atrocities gradually escalated, particularly in Munster with the Desmond rebellions in the second half of the 1500s. The Old English in the Pale, who were predominantly Catholic, also rose up in opposition to English expansionism. Supported by Gaelic chiefs, Viscount Baltinglass, James Eustace, led a revolt in 1580. Baltinglass regarded Queen Elizabeth I as an illegitimate heretic and he was despised by Adam Loftus, the Protestant archbishop of Dublin. An English settler from Yorkshire, Loftus became the first provost of Trinity College. His brother Dudley was granted lands on the Hook Peninsula and so began the Loftus dynasty in the area. Viscount Baltinglass complained about the persecution of Catholics and the policies pursued by Queen Elizabeth I.

Baltinglass partnered with Fiach MacHugh O'Byrne (eulogized in the folk song *Follow Me Up To Carlow*). The O'Byrnes controlled vast lands in south Wicklow and part of County Wexford. They were carrying out raids into the Pale from the south as well as into County Wexford. Anglo-Irish magnates within the Pale such as Viscount Baltinglass were obliged to pay a military tax to finance campaigns against Gaelic lords such as the O'Byrnes. Discontentment was now rife among Dublin's merchants and gentry.

A second Desmond rebellion was mounted in Munster in 1579. The Earl of Desmond, Gerald FitzGerald, took up arms against the Queen. But this was ruthlessly suppressed by the Earl of Ormond, Thomas Butler, on the orders of Elizabeth. In the summer of 1580, Viscount Baltinglass, along with Fiach MacHugh O'Byrne, gathered a rebel force in County Wicklow to assist Desmond. At Glenmalure they killed up to 800 English soldiers in a battle against the Lord Deputy of Ireland, Grey de Wilton. Fighting continued for nearly a year over a large area of the country. The 1632 *Annals of the Four Masters* recorded that "the entire extent of the country from the Slaney to the Shannon and from the Boyne to the meeting of the Three Waters became one scene of strife and dissension." A freelance Papal force of 400 to 500 men, comprising Spanish and Italian, landed at Smerwick on the Dingle Peninsula in County Kerry to assist. But having surrendered to the Lord Deputy's troops, most were slaughtered where they had landed. Queen Elizabeth feared that if Catholicism could unite Anglo-Irishmen from the Pale against the English Crown, the same might happen in England.

The Gaelic clan leader Fiach MacHugh O'Byrne, who successfully fought alongside Viscount Baltinglass in the Battle of Glenmalure in 1580.

Forty-five followers of Baltinglass were hanged in Dublin but he managed to escape to Wexford along with his chaplain, the Wexford-born Jesuit, Father Robert Rochford. From there they hoped to escape to Spain. But their cause was clearly lost and no one wanted to help when they arrived in Wexford in the winter of 1580-1. Finally, a local baker named Matthew Lambert gave them shelter and a group of five sailors tried unsuccessfully to get them passage on a ship. We know the names of four: Robert Meyler, Edward Cheevers, Patrick Cavanagh and John O'Lahy. But Lambert was betrayed and all six were were arrested, imprisoned, and tortured.

According to another Jesuit priest from County Wexford, John Howlin, who published the first account of Irish martyrs in Lisbon in the 1590s, it was summer 1581 before the Lord Deputy, Grey de Wilton, could turn his attention to the south-east. As he made his way down through Wicklow and Gaelic Wexford he had many people hanged under martial law. When he arrived in Wexford town the jail was full of prisoners held on various charges. They included Lambert and the sailors.

The Lord Deputy came to sit as judge in the Wexford trials, the main purpose of which were to strike terror in the people. Howlin recorded that the first to be put on trial was Sir Nicholas Devereux of Ballymagir, situated between Kilmore Quay and Duncormick. A prominent member of the local gentry, Devereux was charged with a capital offence to which he pleaded guilty, but the local jury acquitted him.

Someone had to hang and these would be 'the men of no property.' Matthew Lambert emerged as the spokesman for all six accused of treason. Probably unable to read or write, he was pressed on how he could be loyal to both the Queen and Pope, and said: "I do not know how to debate these things with you. I only want you to know that I am a Catholic and believe in the faith of my holy mother the Catholic Church." The five sailors replied similarly. Their wives and families pleaded for mercy as they were all found guilty of treason and sentenced to be executed by being hanged, drawn and quartered. The sentences on 'The Wexford Martyrs', as they became known, were carried out in the centre of the town on 5 July 1581.

For men convicted of high treason, the statutory penalty was to be hanged, drawn and quartered. The prisoner was tied to a wooden frame and drawn by horse to the place of execution. There he was hanged, almost to the point of death, castrated, disembowelled, beheaded and quartered (chopped into four pieces). His remains were then displayed in a prominent public place to serve as a warning as to the fate of traitors.

Viscount Baltinglass managed to escape to Munster where the Desmond rebellion was still ongoing. After the Earl of Desmond was killed in battle, Baltinglass fled to Spain, where he tried but failed to persuade King Philip II to send an army to assist the Irish rebels. Viscount Baltinglass, James Eustace, died in Spain in 1585.

Blacksmith who worked for 74 years at Ballymitty forge

Johnny Whitty (1917-2008) at work in his forge at Doyle's Cross, Ballymitty in the 1980s. (photo: Paddy Donovan)

BORN IN 1917, Johnny Whitty became an apprentice blacksmith at the forge ideally located on the main Wexford to Wellingtonbridge road at Doyle's Cross, Hilltown, Ballymitty. He began work in 1931 at the age of 14 and continued to labour until finally retiring at the age of 88 in 2006, after a staggering 74 years working in the same forge, one of the few remaining in the country.

According to *Griffith's Valuation* of 1853, there was a blacksmith named John Molloy at the forge at Hilltown. [*Griffith's Valuation* was carried out in Ireland between 1848 and 1864 to determine liability to pay the Poor rate — for the support of the poor and destitute within each Poor Law Union]. John Molloy was followed into the business by his son Myles, followed in turn by his own son Mike, who was born about 1898.

Johnny Whitty was an apprentice to Mike Molloy. When Johnny married Maryann (née Connick) from Murrintown, Mike gave the couple a present of £89 to buy a cottage for themselves at Racks Cross, Harristown, just one-and-a-half miles from the forge. Johnny and Mary remained living in the cottage for the rest of their lives and he worked at the forge from 1931 to 2006.

For centuries, every district had a forge that was a popular meeting place and the blacksmith, who supplied them with their ironwork needs, was well respected. Farm implements and household ironware needs such as gates, hinges and bolts were also produced by the local blacksmith. Horses were used in all transport and farm work and the blacksmith played an important role in the community. The forge was usually sited along busy roads and at crossroads.

Apart from mainly shoeing horses, the blacksmiths of County Wexford were also busy manufacturing pikes in advance of the 1798 rebellion. As soon as they were made they were taken away to hiding places as raids on the forges by the authorities were common. It was said that every blacksmith in the county had taken the United Irishman's oath. The blacksmiths in turn administered the oath to volunteers who wished to enlist. Forges became meeting places for planning the rebellion that began in May 1798. Tens of thousands of pikes were made in the forges of County Wexford and the authorities were well aware of the role played by the blacksmith in the early months of 1798, and so they became marked men. Many forges were burned down by yeomen along with the blacksmiths' dwellings. Some blacksmiths were hanged in Wexford merely on suspicion of manufacturing pikes.

In the mid-1800s County Wexford had about 250 forges, one sited about every three miles from the next, and the villages and towns had several forges to service the community. However, by the end of World War II, the horse was rapidly being replaced by the motorcar and tractor and, though

The 'Wexford pike' was usually about two feet in length and attached to a ten-inch ash handle. The sharp hook was used to cut the girth that kept the saddle in place on a horse and to then pull down the rider.

Johnny Whitty at work in the Ballymitty forge in the early 2000s. (photo: Michael Snoek)

some blacksmiths diversified into wrought-iron work, the roadside forge gradually became a thing of the past, with very few surviving beyond the twentieth century.

The old forge buildings were simple, with thatched roofs or of slate that was introduced in the 19th century. In 1953, the forge at Ballymitty was re-roofed with asbestos sheeting. Coal was the most common fuel that was burned in the forge, with supplies coming from Stafford's of Wexford. Power was supplied by a wind charger until the introduction of rural electrification in the early 1960s. A bellows was used to deliver additional air to the fuel, raising the rate of combustion and therefore the heat output. The old bellows in Ballymitty was replaced with an electric motor fan in 1963. Johnny Whitty bought the forge from the owner, Michael Molloy, in 1974.

Johnny was a highly skilled blacksmith and hugely dedicated to his job, often working from 7am until 9pm. One of his prized tools was a large pipe cutter, brought back to him from America by a local teacher in the 1930s and still in use after 70 years. He was a religious man and would cycle every day to and from the forge and to Mass on Sundays. Johnny was very well respected in the community and was active in all things sportive in Ballymitty. He was involved in Gaelic football and played handball into his 80s. He was president of the Ballymitty Handball Club for many years and had a great love of horses.

Johnny Whitty. (photo: Michael Snoek)

When Johnny Whitty finally retired in 2006 at the age of 88, it was in part to care for his wife Maryann, who died just 18 months before Johnny himself passed away in 2008.

Following the campaign for Catholic emancipation in Ireland, led by Daniel O'Connell, emancipation was finally granted in 1829. St. Peter's Catholic church in Hilltown, Ballymitty was built in 1837 under the aegis of the parish priest, Father Peter Corish. Shortly after the church opened, it was visited by Father L. Fox, an Oblate missionary priest, who was invited to give a lecture to the faithful. Father Fox later wrote an article in the Boston-based *Donahoe's Magazine* reminiscing about his years of missionary life. In it he referred to his visit to Ballymitty. An extract was reproduced by *The People* newspaper in 1905:

St. Peter's Church, Ballymitty.

'Amongst the rural missions in which I took part from time to time, none were more successful than those which were preached to the faithful and patriotic Catholics of Wexford. In Ballymitty the pastor, who was a zealous but eccentric man, had just built a new chapel and he determined to inaugurate its opening by a mission. Among his other peculiarities, he would not have a single window made so that it could be opened, "for" said he, "if the worshippers only minded their prayers they would not care for too much bodily heat, or too little fresh air." The result was that at the very first Mass while I was preaching, first one and then another fainted away. Each one was carried to the sacristy where the excellent parish priest gave a glass of wine to every sufferer. In this way he employed no fewer than three bottles of the altar wine. Dreading that these fainting fits would become contagious, especially with the prospect of a glass of good wine to help to bring them round again, I announced in the evening that anyone who felt that an attack of weakness was coming on should retire at once, without disturbing the congregation and that the pastor would give them a glass of water, as he could not afford to dispense any more wine. But this was not the only device which I adopted to check these attacks and their consequent disturbance. I engaged two young men to provide themselves with long sticks and before the people assembled for the evening service, I went with them all round the chapel and directed them to smash half a dozen small panes of glass, in each of the tall windows. The remedy was extreme but it was effectual, for not a single case of fainting occurred from that time till the close of the mission.'

The popular 'Seisiún Round The Fire' always attracts a large crowd.

Following the death of Johnny Whitty, the forge was purchased by local man Michael Reville. He has since lovingly restored it — complete with a brass bed in the upstairs bedroom, where blacksmiths once slept. Michael wanted to use the building, which oozes character, as a music outlet for his talented children, who all play traditional Irish music. A highly popular *Seisiún Round The Fire,* with an eclectic mix of music and performances, is held in the venue on the last Saturday of every month.

The former forge at Doyle's Cross, Hilltown, Ballymitty. (photo: Des Kiely)

Farmer found murdered on morning of his wedding

SUNDAY, 21 FEBRUARY 1897 was to be 45-year-old James Kelly's big day. A single farmer, he cared for his sick 86-year-old mother — who was deaf and bed-ridden — on their 13-acre farm in the townland of Kilcavan Upper, a few miles north of Gorey. According to a report in the *Irish Times* on Friday, 26 February 1897 under the heading *Shocking Murder in Co. Wexford*, James "by his thrift and successful agricultural operations had amassed, it is believed, considerable savings."

James was one of seven children on the family farm, at the foot of Tara Hill and located in an isolated part of north Wexford. Their father died when he was only 4 years old and their mother continued to work the farm with the help of neighbours. The years rolled by, his brother Martin married and settled down and his five sisters had moved on, three of them marrying farmers in the locality. James remained with his mother and was known to be an extremely hard worker, inoffensive, fair in his dealings and careful with his money.

Their house was a humble, single-storey thatched cottage and according to the 1901 census, there were only five households in the immediate area.

His nearest neighbours were the Friths, who lived on the far side of the road. Mary Frith (née Doyle) was a widow, and an "heiress to a considerable amount of property", according to the *Irish Times* report and whom James planned to marry. She lived with her elderly widowed mother, Mary Doyle. James's marriage to Mary Frith was delayed "owing to some cause or another" and the ceremony was delayed by two days until Tuesday, 23 February.

On the day before the wedding, his fiancée Mary went to Enniscorthy with her eldest son. James's nephew, 12-year-old Moses, worked in the fields with him and helped out around the house. He prepared some potatoes in a pot above the hearth for his uncle that evening and left shortly after 8pm. James accompanied him as far as the house of a neighbour, Charlie Noctor, about a quarter of a mile away. Moses picked up some candles from Noctor for James, who took them and wished the young boy goodnight. James returned home and sat by candlelight in front of the fire in his kitchen while his mother lay in bed in the adjoining room.

When Moses returned the next morning at 8.30am he found his uncle lying on his side on the floor in a pool of blood with his feet in the hearth. The stool he had been sitting on was partly under him, the kitchen window was smashed and there were marks made by shotgun pellets on the wall. He ran across the road to Mary Frith, the bride-to-be, to alert her. She hurried to the house, followed by her mother. The young boy then ran a half a mile to James's brother-in-law Ned Doyle, who got the news to Moses' father, who alerted

A three-window thatched cottage similar to James Kelly's in Kilcavan. (photo: Irish Examiner)

the police in Coolgreany. When Moses returned he found Mary Frith alone and noticed the stool had been moved away from under the body.

Martin Kelly, the dead man's brother, arrived at the cottage at about 10 o'clock and the police came soon after, followed by the acting District Inspector Kelly and Head Constable O'Halloran, travelling from Gorey and Wexford. However, before the police arrived, the kitchen had been tidied up and the yard outside swept in anticipation of the visitors' arrival. Any possibility of finding footprints in the yard were now gone but the Head Constable carefully examined the house into the night hours. Boxes in James' bedroom containing money had been broken open and other hiding places emptied of his savings. It appeared the killer was well acquainted with the house.

News of the killing spread quickly around the county and beyond. A large number of police were on hand the next morning as the coroner for Wexford, Dr. D. T. Murphy, was expected to arrive from Wexford at Gorey station on the 4.30pm train. A crowd of men, who were hastily selected and summoned to serve on the jury at the inquest, waited on the road adjoining the house. As a result of some bungling by officials, they were informed, much to their annoyance, that the coroner could not make the journey until the following day. James Kelly's corpse had to lie in the same position for another day and "preservatives had to be requisitioned to prevent the corruption of the remains", according to the *Enniscorthy Guardian* on Saturday, 27 February 1897.

Dr. Murphy arrived on the midday train on Thursday and jury members entered the house as their names were called by the coroner. After the body was formally examined, the jurors were moved to Mrs Frith's house across the road, where a room had been prepared for the proceedings. They were sworn in, the inquest commenced and the District Inspector and Head Constable questioned the witnesses. Finally, the coroner concluded that "... from the evidence we believe death resulted from injury to the brain, caused by a gun shot wound wilfully inflicted by some person or persons unknown." This was accepted by the jury without hesitation and the coroner, having thanked them, concluded the proceedings.

Four weeks later, on 23 March 1897, at the conclusion of the opening day of the spring session in Wexford Courthouse, Mr. Justice William Johnson remarked: "If there was nothing more, I should simply stop here, but I regret very much to say that it has been reported to me by the constabulary that your county has been stained by a foul murder, committed last February. A man, whose wedding was to have taken place the next day, was shot dead through the window of his own house, there being no inmate except for himself and his poor old mother, who was unable to offer any assistance. For that crime no one has yet been made amenable, and, therefore, I offer no further observations upon it."

A short follow-up article appeared in the *Enniscorthy Guardian* two months later: "Strange allegations are again rife relative to the murder of James Kelly at Kilcavan in February last. The police have been untiring in their efforts to trace the murderer, and it is stated that while they know perfectly well who the person is, yet more evidence is required to warrant an arrest and to substantiate the charge. Peculiar developments are expected in a short time, which, should they come to pass, will inevitably land the murderer in the dock. An absurd rumour has been set afloat that the house of the murdered man is haunted by a ghostly visitant. This, of course, is a pure concoction, the emanation and vagary of a sensation monger. To the minds of the people of the locality, horror-struck as they were by the awful crime perpetuated in their midst, the rumour carried a thrill of the terror and superstition that still attaches credence to the wild tale."

Nobody was ever arrested for the murder.

Wexford Courthouse stood on Commercial Quay. Completed in 1808, it replaced the old courthouse in the Bullring. Most of this building was destroyed in an arson attack by the IRA in 1921 during the War of Independence. (photo: National Library of Ireland)

Witchcraft in Wexford – the case of the invisible weasel

AN EXTRACT from the Wexford Petty Sessions in September 1830. The petty sessions were held by justices of the peace, who were lay people. A schoolmaster named Donnelly was charged before it with witchcraft and the plaintiff was a tailor called Knox. The following report appeared in *The Wexford Herald* at the time and was reprinted in *The Journal of Law, The Literary Gazette* and *The London and Paris Observer,* among others:

EDWARD SUTTON, THOMAS WALKER, and WILMSDEN RICHARDS, Esqrs. on the bench.

As soon as the magistrates had taken their seats, a school master by the name of Donnelly, stepped up to the bench, and searching his pockets, said he had to submit to the magistrates a summons the most extraordinary which had ever been issued since the days of Joan of Arc, and he wished to know if he was to be detained there from his business at the instance of a person who was deranged.

Mr. WALKER, after looking at the summons, said that Knox, (the plantiff,) had a right to summon him on such a charge, extraordinary as it might appear. He hoped, however, that his (Donnelly's) wife was not in court, as there was no necessity for her attendance.

Donnelly said he did not let her come.

Donnelly's wife and daughter were included in the summons.

Mr. WALKER said that magistrates were bound by their commissions to inquire into all cases of witchcraft. (In a low tone.) Is he here? Perhaps we might settle it without inquiry.

Knox here made his appearance by the side of Donnelly. He was an active looking man, of the middle size, with a dark visage, and about forty years of age. There was no very peculiar wildness depicted in his countenance. Having been desired to state the circumstances as briefly as he could, he asked was Donnelly sworn?

Mr. WALKER said he was not, and perhaps it would not be necessary. If any one was to be sworn, it would be himself. What was the charge?

Knox—Witching, your worship, real witching—(laughter.) And here is a letter which I wish you would read, but it is too long.

Was this letter written by the witch?—No, it was written by myself; but it would be too long to read it all. Read it there, (folding the letter,) from that part down.

Mr. WALKER declined reading it.

Clerk of the Court—State all the facts now, and nothing else.

Knox hesitated some time.

Mr. WALKER—What was it that occurred?—Let him be sworn, or let me be sworn, and let him deny it, if he can, that he keeps it in his house, and that I have heard it every day, and every night, and every hour, and every minute, and every other time—(laughter.)

Have you seen it?—No, I never saw it; but I heard it, and that five minutes before I came here, speaking as plain as I do now—(laughter.)

What is it you heard?—A weasel—(loud and continued laughter,) or something, I don't know what it is; but (turning to Donnelly, whose risible faculties were evidently in motion,) I heard him say it was a weasel a hundred times—(laughter.) It knows all my thoughts, and every thing that I do—(loud laughter.) I'm quite certain of that. And it knows what I am speaking, even at this moment—(laughter.)

Does it cut your cloth? (Knox is a tailor.) No, it does not.

Does it do you any harm?—Yes, it annoys my mind. It is not a pleasant thing to have my thoughts known. I am sure no one would like it.

Have you ever any thoughts that you would not wish it should know?—Yes, perhaps I have. I am a freemason, and it would get the secret from me if it could—(loud laughter.)

But it was never able to get that from you?—It endeavoured to do it, but I kept upon my guard—(loud laughter.)

Mr. WALKER—Well, I would strongly advise you, if you have any thoughts which you wish to keep secret, to have a guard over them in future.

Knox—I could not be always on my guard.

Mr. WALKER—If Mr. Donnelly promises it shall not annoy you in future, will that satisfy you?—Knox made no answer.

Donnelly said he would do every thing in his power to satisfy him.

Knox—(tossing his head and speaking in an under tone.)—Oh! that is all nonsense—there's a mystery in it.

Donnelly said he was very certain he would still be annoyed by the plaintiff, for, when the case would be dismissed in this court, he (Knox,) would immediately bring it into the mayor's office, and bring him before the mayor also—(laughter.)

Knox—I will, into all the offices of the united kingdom—(laughter.)

Mr. WALKER (to Donnelly)—Well, you have only to send word to the different magistrates that you have destroyed the weasel.

Knox—It knows all my thoughts, and knows the thoughts of many other persons in Wexford also.

Mr. WALKER said the case must be dismissed as it then stood, but recommended Knox to employ an attorney, and then bring the case before them, when they might be able to decide in his favour.

Knox—Is there no law to punish a man for such an annoyance?

Mr. WALKER—We cannot afford you redress, as the act of parliament relative to witchcraft has been abolished.

Knox—Then why not abolish the witches also?—(Bursts of laughter.)

Mr. WALKER observed that the case must be dismissed.

Knox said he would go from Wexford to Dublin, and from Dublin to Carrickfergus, and from Carrickfergus to London, and lay the entire case before the duke of Leinster—(loud laughter.)

Mr. Cooper remarked that it was a very deplorable case. He (Knox,) ought to get a few pet rats and let them loose where the weasel is, and when the weasel comes out, knock him down with a goose—(laughter.)

Mr. RICHARDS asked Knox, when did he hear the weasel the first time?

Knox answered a twelvemonth ago.

Mr. RICHARDS asked him, had he any quarrel with Donnelly?

He said he had not.

The forgotten Anglo-Norman settlement of Carrig

The location of the 12th century Carrig Castle and borough of Carrig. The Crimean Monument round tower was built on the same site in 1858. (from a 1976 photo courtesy of John Ironside)

THE FIRST Anglo- or Cambro-Norman stronghold in Ireland was established at Carrig, located on a strategic promontory on the southern side of the River Slaney estuary, just a few miles north-west of Wexford town. Robert FitzStephen, the Welsh warrior knight who landed with the first wave of Anglo-Norman invaders at Bannow Bay in 1169, hastily built a circular fortification or 'ringwork', probably of earth and timber, at this location.

ROBERT FITZSTEPHEN

Robert was born in about 1120 to Nesta, the only daughter of the last ruler of the southern Welsh kingdom of Deheubarth and one of the most famous women from Wales during the medieval period. She was a beauty and a lover of Henry I of England and she even bore him a son, Henry FitzRoy. In 1105 she married a knight named Gerald de Windsor, who was appointed Constable of Pembroke. Their third son was Maurice FitzGerald. After Gerald de Windsor died in 1118, Nesta married Stephen, Constable of Cardigan. Their son was Robert FitzStephen.

In Old French, which the Normans brought with them from Normandy to England in 1066, *Fitz* meant 'son of' from the word *fils* (son), thus FitzStephen was the son of Stephen. In Ireland, some Irish names were Anglo-Normanized, such as FitzPatrick.

The medieval historian Giraldus Cambrensis (Gerald of Wales), a nephew of Maurice FitzGerald, described his half-brother Robert as being "stout in person, with a handsome countenance, and in stature somewhat above the middle height; he was bountiful, generous, and pleasant, but too fond of wine and women. An excellent man – the true pattern of singular courage and unparalleled enterprise."

Diarmait Mac Murchada was dispossessed of the powerful kingdom of Leinster, which he had held since 1126, by the new High King, Rory O'Connor. He fled to Britain and travelled to Acquitaine in France and sought the assistance of Henry II to win back his kingdom. Henry had married Eleanor of Aquitaine in 1152 and as king and queen created an Anglo-French empire that stretched from Scotland to the Pyrenees. Henry was not willing to intervene personally in Ireland but instead gave Diarmait permission to recruit mercenaries from among his Norman knights. The most obvious place to go for recruits was south Wales, where the Welsh princes had been slowly reclaiming their lands back from the Norman invaders who had seized them 100 years earlier. Robert FitzStephen, who had become dispossessed, and his older half-brother Maurice FitzGerald, agreed to accompany Mac Murchada to Ireland. In return he promised to grant them 100,000 acres in the two cantreds (later baronies) of Forth and Bargy and control of Wexford town.

SIEGE OF WEXFORD

According to Gerald of Wales' *Expugnatio Hibernica (Conquest of Ireland)*, written in Latin in 1189, Robert arrived at Bannow with a force of about 400 knights and archers on 1 May 1169, accompanied by Strongbow's uncle, Hervey de Montmorency. They joined an army of about 500 under Diarmait Mac Murchada. The first minor Anglo-Norman battle on Irish soil took place at Duncormick and together they continued their march on the town of Wexford. The defenders located inside the then wooden defensive walls of Wexford numbered about 2,000 but the Norse-Irish town fell after two days. It is recorded that 18 Normans and 3 defenders died on the first day in the Siege of Wexford. On the second day FitzStephen ordered the burning of all ships in the harbour. The Irish defenders, persuaded by two bishops, finally surrendered, swearing allegiance to Diarmait.

Later in 1169, Robert FitzStephen's half-brother Maurice FitzGerald sailed into Wexford from Wales with two ships and 140 armed followers. Along with Diarmait Mac Murchada's force, they marched towards Dublin and laid waste to its hinterland. Robert remained in Wexford where he applied himself to the settlement of the town. He now felt safe enough to bring his wife and children to Ireland and began to reinforce his stronghold at Carrig.

On 23 August 1170, Richard de Clare ('Strongbow'), who had been deprived of the earldom of Pembroke, arrived at Passage with the promise of Diarmait's daughter Aoife's hand in marriage and the prospect of succeeding to Leinster on Diarmait's death. He married Aoife two days later in Christ Church Cathedral in Waterford. Strongbow carried out an assault on Waterford and, along with forces of Diarmait, took Dublin on 21 September. When Diarmait died suddenly (and conveniently) in May 1171, Strongbow declared himself king of Leinster. Diarmait was buried in Ferns Cathedral, where what is believed to be his gravestone can be seen in the outer graveyard.

The High King, Ruaidrí Ua Conchobair (Rory O'Connor), then launched an attack on the Anglo-Normans in Dublin. There followed a two-month siege

Illustrations of Robert FitzStephen and his half-brother Maurice FitzGerald from the 1189 manuscript Expugnatio Hibernica, an account of the 1169 invasion of Ireland written by Maurice's nephew, Gerald of Wales. He saw the Irish as backward and barbarian and claimed that they preferred axes to swords or bows.

and Robert FitzStephen sent an elite contingent of thirty-six of his troops from Carrig to help the Anglo-Norman garrison in Dublin. This left FitzStephen's remaining force of only five knights and a handful of archers exposed. They subsequently came under attack in Wexford from the local Irish and fled to their fortress at Carrig.

Strongbow negotiated with the High King and proposed that the Anglo-Normans keep all lands they had conquered and in return would acknowledge him as overlord. But O'Connor would only agree to them keeping Dublin, Waterford and Wexford. Strongbow's army carried out a surprise attack on O'Connor's troops at Castleknock, killing hundreds, with O'Connor surrendering. But the Irish brought bishops to Carrig who, swearing on relics that their information was true, told FitzStephen that Maurice FitzGerald and Dublin had instead fallen to Rory O'Connor and so tricked him into surrendering. When news came that Strongbow was on his way to Wexford, the Irish burnt Wexford and fled to Begerin Island (now part of the North Slobs), taking with them FitzStephen and a number of hostages. Strongbow did not carry out an attack on the island, fearing that FitzStephen and the other hostages would be executed. Robert FitzStephen, now in his fifties, remained a prisoner in chains.

INVASION BY HENRY II

On 17 October 1171, King Henry II invaded Ireland with an armada of 400 ships, landing at Waterford. He was the first king of England to set foot on Irish soil. He wanted to limit the growing power of the Anglo-Norman lords, including Strongbow, who had begun to colonize much of Leinster. He claimed in a papal bull that he was authorized to conquer Ireland to reform the Irish Church and bring Irish society into line with the moral standards of the rest of Christian Europe.

King Henry II invaded Ireland in 1171 and declared himself overlord.

FitzStephen was taken from his cell on Begerin Island and marched to Waterford, where he was presented to the king. Now called a traitor and a criminal, having initiated the Norman invasion of

Ireland, he was incarcerated in Reginald's Tower. But after just a few weeks he was pardoned and probably accompanied the king on his triumphant march on Dublin, where he spent the next six months. Henry declared himself 'overlord of Ireland' and accepted the submissions of the Irish kings. He declared Dublin, Waterford and Wexford to be crown lands but allowed Strongbow to hold the remainder of Leinster and Meath, on condition he held them in feudal service to him. Robert FitzStephen was for a time put on garrison duty on Dublin's walls.

Henry left Ireland in April 1172, leaving the High King Rory O'Connor as his vassal and he as overlord. The Anglo-Normans held one quarter of the country under Strongbow and his heirs. Robert FitzStephen, who had rehabilitated himself in Henry's service, was given the right to the kingdom of Desmond in Cork, jointly with Milo de Cogan, another Anglo-Norman knight from Glamorgan.

Strongbow died in Dublin in 1176 and was buried in Christ Church and Maurice FitzGerald died in Wexford in the same year. Milo de Cogan was killed in 1182 and Robert FitzStephen finally returned to Wales, where is believed to have died in 1183. His lands eventually fell to Robert's half-sister's son, Philip de Barri, who had landed with him at Bannow in 1169, bringing the name Barry to Ireland. He had also taken part in the Siege of Wexford.

Strongbow's daughter, 17-year-old Isabel, married the English knight William Marshal, aged 43, in London in 1189. William succeeded as Lord of Leinster, acquiring most of counties Kilkenny, Carlow and Wexford. They made Kilkenny their base and established Kilkenny Castle as well as Ferns Castle and Tintern Abbey. They also founded the successful port town of New Ross and commissioned the construction of the Tower of Hook to protect shipping to the town through Waterford Harbour. William and Isabel had five sons and five daughters and he became known as the 'greatest knight that ever lived'.

The lands colonized by the Anglo-Normans were divided into small holdings. Some were held by knights, who in turn were obliged to perform military service for their overlord. The urban centres of Wexford and Ferns were expanded by the Anglo-Normans and the town of Enniscorthy was founded. New boroughs were established at Bannow, Gorey, Courtown, Clonmines, Taghmon, Fethard, Old Ross and Carrig.

THE TOWN OF CARRIG

Carrig developed around the castle in the 13th century and at one time consisted of about 110 dwellings, two mills and a ferry linking the north shore of the Slaney at Ferrycarrig ('the ferry to Carrig'). A stone castle at Carrig was first recorded in 1231. Carrig's parish church of St. Nicholas of Myra and grave-yard were located a half mile south of Carrig Castle and close to a holy well. Only a very small section of the 600-year-old church walls remains but the

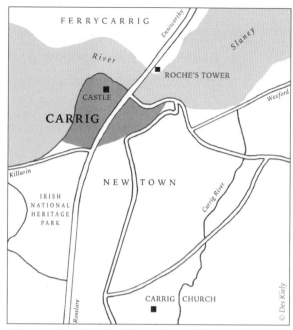

The approximate location of the new borough of Carrig that gave the townland the name Newtown.

graveyard is still in use and holds many victims from both sides of the 1798 Rebellion. The river that runs close by was immortalized in the song *Carrig River*, written in 1890 by James 'Messa' Nolan and James 'Shaw' McGrath, both from Hill Street in Wexford. It mentions Carrig graveyard in the lines:

It's often that with vain regret we think on things we've seen
We've seen the past but can't forget and mourn what might have been
As we strolled along the sweet birds' song was ringing in the sky
O'er the lonely graves of Carrig where our '98 men lie.

The entrance to Carrig graveyard with a plaque to victims of 1798 who are buried within. (photos: Des Kiely)

DECLINE

William Marshal II died in 1231 and within fourteen years all five of his sons died, leaving no male heirs. The lordship of Leinster eventually became weakened, with land ownership patterns fragmented. The disenfranchised native Irish had bided their time and now some were seeking protection money from the colonizers. Many of the Anglo-Norman settlers and their descendants were leaving Ireland to fight in the king's wars and food was being exported from Ireland to supply the troops overseas. A Gaelic resurgence was now unrestrained. By the late 1200s, large numbers of settlers had been evicted or killed.

By the 1320s the Irish were in control again of much of the north of County Wexford and the Hiberno-Norman colonists, as they were now known, were gone from the region by the end of the century and were now mainly confined to the southern baronies of Forth, Bargy and Shelburne. This area south of Forth Mountain was afforded a natural defence by the sea on the west, south and east and became increasingly isolated from the Gaelic north, as evidenced by the survival of the Yola dialect into the 19th century.

The settlement of Carrig was in decline in the early 14th century and Carrig Castle was already in ruins in 1324. The ferry was now in the hands of the Roches, who built tower houses at Barntown and at Ferrycarrig to control river traffic along the Slaney and the ferry crossing. Richard FitzGodbert de Roche was the first Norman knight to land in Ireland in 1167.

Stones from the castle are recorded as having been used in the construction of nearby Belmont House, about a half mile to the south but no longer standing. It was built for the Earl of Donoughmore in about 1800. Remaining stones were used in the construction of the replica round tower erected 'in memory of the officers, non-commissioned officers and men of the County Wexford who lost their lives in the Crimea during the war with Russia 1854-56.' The tower was built on the site of 'the ancient fort of Carrig' and the land was donated by the Earl of Donoughmore, Richard Hely-Hutchinson, and completed in 1858.

The Dublin Wicklow and Wexford Railway Company was responsible for the extension of the Dublin-Enniscorthy route to Wexford and by 1871 the line had reached Carcur, where they opened a temporary train station. The railway line and tunnel ran through the parish of Carrig.

EXCAVATIONS

In the late 1970s, Wexford County Council acquired the land where the borough of Carrig once stood, as well the adjoining marshland to the south-east along the Slaney. This was to facilitate the building of an extension of the N11 national primary road, bypassing Wexford town as far as the Rosslare Road. However, instead of opting for a high-level bridge across the river, the old borough of Carrig was to be dissected, separating the site of the original Carrig castle from the location of the rest of the settlement. A new bridge over the Slaney opened in October 1980 and the huge task of cutting through the rock began in 1981. That took about two years to complete and the bypass, traversing the railway and running as far as Whitford, was completed in 1988.

Archaeological excavations were conducted at the time at the location of the ringwork and castle but not within the road catchment – a site of major archaeological significance. Foundations and pits were obliterated, according to labourers who worked on the site. The first archaeological excavations at the site of the ringfort were undertaken in 1984, with more carried out in 1986. Significant findings were made but the site again became overgrown and generally forgotten.

The marshy land to the west of the new roadway was developed as the Irish

The N11 Wexford bypass was cut through the site of the medieval settlement of Carrig in the early 1980s. The 15th century Roche tower is on the left. (photo: Paddy Donovan)

National Heritage Park and opened to the public in 1987. The park tells the 9,000-year history of human settlement in Ireland, from the Mesolithic period to the Anglo-Norman invasion. It attracts about 70,000 visitors annually. A reconstructed Norman ringfort was built close to the site of the original Carrig ringwork – then a wooden structure and later stone castle.

The Roche tower house was built on the northern side of the Slaney to control river traffic and the ferry crossing.
(from a 1976 photo courtesy of John Ironside)

The *Digging the Lost Town of Carrig* project was set up by the Irish Archaeology Field School in association with the Irish National Heritage Park. The first groups of international students arrived on site in January and July 2018 to take part in the first four-week dig seasons at the Carrig ringwork site. The 1980s digs were re-exposed and re-recorded. New excavations have been carried out to access the original 12th century defences and 13th/14th century stone buildings. Parts of a large external ditch, measuring 2m deep and 5m wide with a 2m-high bank have been exposed. Post-holes in the interior of the ringwork, possibly representing some of the first Anglo-Norman structures in Ireland, were also discovered.

To mark the 850th anniversary of the construction of the first Anglo-Norman fortification in Ireland, built in the autumn of 1169 at Carrig, a two-day international conference, *Carrig 850*, was held in October 2019 in the Irish National Heritage Park. Investigative excavations of the site are expected to continue for several years.

The archaeology students' Digging the Lost Town of Carrig project in summer 2018. (photo: Des Kiely)

Beaten to death in Crossabeg over delay in paying wages

The farmhouse of Frank and Lizzie Reck on Cushanna Lane in the townland of Crory, Crossabeg.

THE BLOOD-COVERED corpse of Lizzie Reck was found lying in a ditch just 300 yards from her farm gate at Crory, about a mile from Crossabeg, on the morning of 10 July 1931. Her brother Frank had earlier beaten off her killer, 58-year-old farm labourer Henry Carty, in a fight with him a short time earlier. It later transpired that Carty's anger may have been triggered by a delay in being paid 3 shillings and sixpence in wages that was owed to him. The killing shocked the people of Wexford ninety years ago.

Farmer Frank Reck, aged 70, lived with his 65-year-old sister Lizzie on their 40-acre farm. Carty, a former soldier in the British Army, lived about half a mile away from the Recks, in the townland of Ballyboggan. He had worked for them occasionally as a casual labourer and for five weeks prior to the killing, they employed him as a farm labourer for a wage of 10 shillings a week and that included his meals.

Henry Carty arrived at the Reck farm by horse and cart at around 8.15am on Friday, 10 July. Frank Reck was in the farmyard with a neighbour named John Culleton, who had come for the loan of a grubber or cultivator. All three then loaded the implement onto a cart and as Culleton was leaving, Frank told Carty to go into the house to have his breakfast, which his sister Lizzie had prepared for him, as was the custom. Frank accompanied Culleton up the laneway from the house as far as the public road. He then went into his hayshed across the road and tied down a few haycocks in the adjoining field.

Frank returned to his farmyard about twenty minutes later. In the meantime, his sister Lizzie had milked one cow in the cowshed and was looking after some fowl, while Carty was having breakfast in the house. Frank called Carty and asked him to hurry up as he needed him to accompany him to Crossabeg to get some pigs weighed. He proceeded to let the pigs out of the sty and drove them down the lane towards the public road. When Carty caught up with him, there was a silence between the two men. With Carty walking on Frank's right-hand side, they turned right onto the public road without speaking and headed towards the village. To break the silence, Frank asked Carty if he could guess the weight of the pigs. Carty made no reply.

When the pair had continued about 200 yards along the road, Frank received a violent blow to the side of his face from a heavy instrument, which knocked him to the ground. While he was down, Carty kicked him in the mouth, knocking out some teeth and delivered a blow to the side of his head. Frank managed to get to his feet and beat off Carty by hitting him with his

Garda Dwyer from Castlebridge barracks and Frank Reck outside the farmhouse. The walking stick that Reck used to defend himself is seen next to him.

walking stick and throwing some stones at him as he ran back towards the house. Carty caught up with him and tried to bite him as they both fell to the ground. Frank held him under the chin to stop him biting. They both got up again and as they got further down the road Carty ran to get loose stones. Frank managed to trip him up and when he fell put his foot on his throat. He then tried to climb a fence into a field to find a shortcut home. As Carty pursued him, Frank struck him again with his stick with full force to the head and Carty fell back.

When Frank reached the house he told Lizzie what had just happened and said she should go to the house of their neighbour William Shiggins, an insurance agent who lived about quarter of a mile away, to alert him. When Shiggins was told of the fight

The spot, about 300 yards from the gate to her home, where the body of Lizzie Reck was found.

between Frank and Carty, he left on his bicycle for the garda barracks in Castlebridge, to report the assault. About ten minutes after her husband had left to alert the gardaí, Mrs. Shiggins saw Carty passing her house and his face was covered in blood. When William Shiggins reached the barracks, he and Sergeant Bernard Keating left at about 10.50am to cycle back to Crory.

In the meantime, the local postman, Michael Neville, in the company of Martin Brien, was cycling along Crory Lane towards Castlebridge. They came across a woman lying at the side of the road about 300 yards beyond the gate to the Recks' farmhouse. They could see a gaping hole in her jaw with blood on her face and around her mouth. Neville took her right hand and said to Brien that she was dead. He told Brien to remain there while he called to Mrs. Shiggins' house. He shouted to some men working in a local quarry that there a body on the road. One of them, John Murphy, said he would fetch a priest.

On his way, Murphy met Sergeant Keating and William Shiggins and told them about the body. The sergeant gave him directions to the priest's house and instructed him to also have a doctor sent out. A short distance later they came upon Henry Carty walking in the direction of Castlebridge. He was covered in blood, from his head to his boots. 'I'm going to Castlebridge to give myself up at the barracks; I've killed Lizzie Reck,' he said. 'Surely you didn't kill her,' said the sergeant. 'I have done a job on her; she's as dead as a stone,' said Carty.

Sergeant Keating told Shiggins to continue on to Crory to check out Carty's story. After Shiggins left, the sergeant asked Carty why he killed her. 'She was cogaring [whispering] about me all day,' he said. 'How did you kill her?', asked the sergeant. 'With my hands and boots,' he replied. When Shiggins returned and said he had seen the body, Sergeant Keating told him to continue ahead of them to the barracks, while he escorted Carty there. Passing the house of Bridget Kehoe, she asked 'What's up?'. 'I fought with Frank and knocked Lizzie out,' said Carty.

The case was heard in Wexford District Court on 22 July 1931. Henry Carty stood accused of the murder of Lizzie Reck and the attempted murder of her brother Frank. Detective-Sergeant James Harmon gave evidence that he attended the scene of the murder on 10 July and searched for a possible implement that might have been used in the killing, but found nothing. He then went on to the Reck home and there saw the body covered in a sheet in

The postman, Michael Neville, who, along with Martin Brien, discovered the body.

the kitchen, where it had been moved to. He returned to the barracks in Castlebridge where Carty was being held. Examining the accused's clothing, he found his boots and socks were saturated with blood. He stated that his left boot 'contained about a glass of blood.' There were silver-grey hairs stuck to both boots. He had a lock of the deceased's hair cut off and handed this along with Carty's clothes over to the State Pathologist, Dr. John McGrath.

Superintendent Walsh told the court that when Carty was charged and cautioned, the accused said, 'I did not do it wilfully. You are going to hang me. I know what you want. You want information but you won't get it.' When Carty was moved to the barracks on George's Street in Wexford town, he was also charged with the attempted murder of Frank Reck. To the charge he said: 'I never did the like.'

Frank Reck stated that some days before his sister's death, Carty had asked him for wages that were owed to him and they amounted to 3 shillings and sixpence. He said he got the money to give Carty but lost it before he could hand it over. He said he later handed Carty a ten-shilling note to get changed so that he could be paid the

John Murphy, the quarry worker, who went in search of a priest and doctor.

3 shillings and sixpence, but that Carty refused to go for the change. Frank claimed that his sister found the money later.

John Kehoe from Ballyboggan made a sworn statement to the court that on a date before the murder he, Frank Reck and Henry Carty were helping a neighbour, Michel Culleton, with his hay. When their work was finished, Kehoe said he went back to Culleton's house with the accused. Carty remarked to him, 'Frank does things queer; he went to Crossabeg for coal, he lost the money and the coal.' He said that money was due to him for wages.

Garda Dwyer from Castlebridge gave evidence that on the day of the murder, he examined the dead woman's bedroom. He found it had been ransacked and appeared as if somebody had been looking for money.

Henry Carty was moved to Mounjoy Prison in Dublin to await trial. At the subsequent hearing before Mr. Justice Sullivan in the Central Criminal Court, a jury was sworn in and asked to decide if the accused was capable of standing trial. The only witness called was Dr. Hackett from Mountjoy, who had had Carty under close supervision. He told the court that in his opinion the accused was a man of very low mentality. The judge directed the jury to find that the prisoner was deemed unfit to stand trial. He ordered that Carty be kept in custody 'at the pleasure of the Governor-General.' Presumably he was committed to a lunatic asylum.

Dialect that survived for 700 years in Bargy and Forth

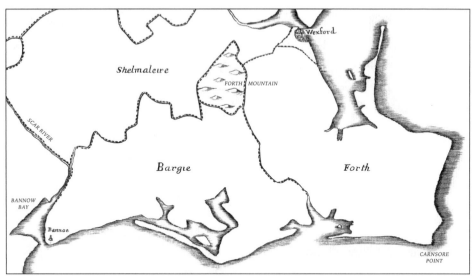

The baronies of south-east Wexford, adapted from William Petty's 1685 map, also known as the 'Down Survey'.

THE DIALECT OF Forth and Bargy, known as Yola *(old)*, was spoken in these baronies following the Anglo-Norman invasion in 1169 until the mid-1800s. Up to then, Middle Irish or *An Mheán-Ghaeilge* was the language spoken in Ireland, after which it began to evolve into Modern Irish. Middle English was introduced into the country for the first time with the arrival of the Anglo-Normans in the kingdom of Uí Cheinnselaig, which is substantially represented today by the county of Wexford.

A hundred years earlier in 1066, an army of Norman, Breton, French and Flemish soldiers, led by the Duke of Normandy, invaded and occupied England. The Duke, from Falaise, became the first Norman King of England and was named William I. The Norman-French language was adopted as the language of the elite for the next 300 years and the language of the common people developed into Middle English – a mixture of Old English with the adoption of some Norman-French vocabulary.

The Anglo- and Cambro-Normans who conquered Ireland came from southern Wales and the Bristol Channel region and spoke a cocktail of languages including Norman-French, Middle English, Welsh and Flemish. In time, these Anglo-Norman settlers around Dublin, Cork, Kilkenny and south

Wexford spoke Middle English and adopted English law. But in the provinces they spoke the native Irish language and embraced Irish law, music and culture, becoming 'more Irish than the Irish themselves'.

The area of south-east Wexford, later known as Forth and Bargy, soon became multi-ethnic. In a charter issued in 1180 by the knight Raymond FitzStephen, who had landed at Bannow, he began by declaring: "to all present and future, French, English, Flemish, Welsh and Irish..." Another knight, Maurice FitzGerald, in describing the new settlers in South Wexford wrote: "they were Irish to the English, and English to the Irish."

Throughout the first century of Anglo-Norman colonization and the imposition of their medieval feudal system, settlers were attracted to this country with offers of land and an improved social status. Some were assigned estates where the Anglo-Normans first landed – a triangle of land between Bannow Bay, Wexford town and Carnsore Point. It was then an isolated area of south-east Ireland, bounded by Forth Mountain to the north and the Scar river to the west. Here the arcane dialect of Yola evolved among their descendants. In the mid-17th century the area was described as the 'Wexford Pale', such was the enduring influence of the colonists.

The Anglo-Normans were the masters of their conquered country, building forts and castles while those who followed were their artisans. It is said that it was more of a marriage than a conquest in this part of Wexford, where landlord and tenant lived in peaceful coexistence. The new settlers were hard-working, and cultivated the then wooded areas of Forth and Bargy. They were a peaceful and industrious people and agrarian trouble was virtually unknown. They rarely travelled any further north than Wexford town. In Shaw Mason's *Parochial Survey of Ireland* in 1814, the story is related of "a Forth woman who happened, once in her life, to wander to the top of the Mountain [their only mountain], and was so overwhelmed by the vast extent of the world which lay to the north of her own, that she resolved never to venture on the appalling prospect any more."

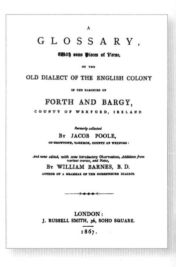

A
GLOSSARY,
With some Pieces of Verse,
OF THE
OLD DIALECT OF THE ENGLISH COLONY
IN THE BARONIES OF
FORTH AND BARGY,
COUNTY OF WEXFORD, IRELAND

Formerly collected
By JACOB POOLE,
OF GROWTOWN, TAGHMON, COUNTY OF WEXFORD:

And now edited, with some Introductory Observations, Additions from various sources, and Notes,
By WILLIAM BARNES, B. D.
AUTHOR OF A GRAMMAR OF THE DORSETSHIRE DIALECT

LONDON:
J. RUSSELL SMITH, 36, SOHO SQUARE.
1867.

Title page of William Barnes' 1867 book that features Jacob Poole's short vocabulary of the Forth and Bargy dialect.

The military surveyor Charles Vallancey (left) and the Dorset poet William Barnes, whose research contributed to the Yola glossary published in 1867.

According to the 19th century Dublin publisher Richard Webb, the dialect died out in the barony of Bargy in the 1700s but in the early 1800s remained the mother tongue along the extreme south-east coast of Forth, especially in the parish of Carne. An uncle of Webb was Jacob Poole, a Quaker farmer and amateur anthropologist from Growtown, just west of Forth Mountain. Poole died in 1827, leaving behind a glossary of about 1,200 Forth and Bargy words in manuscript form. The Dorset poet William Barnes, who in 1863 wrote the *Glossary of the Dorset Dialect*, published the manuscript, with additional words added from other sources, in *A Glossary of the Old Dialect of the English Colony in the Baronies of Forth and Bargy* in 1867. He added about fifty words from the military surveyor Charles Vallencey and a further fifty were contributed by Dr. Charles Russell, President of St. Patrick's College, Maynooth. Additional words were added from an article on Weiseforde (Wexford) and its people and language written by Richard Stanyhurst in his *Description of Ireland* (1577). Richard Webb claimed that he met the last speaker of the dialect, Martin Parle of Carnesore Point, who was born about 1776 and died aged nearly 90 in 1865.

It had been thought that they were speaking a Wessex dialect from Devon or Somerset due to the strong West English tinge. But they also assimilated words and phrases from the local Irish language, such as *poag* (a kiss), *gorsoon* (a lad) and *pucane* (a goat). As in Flemish, as well as in the old Devon and Somerset dialects, words beginning with 's' were pronounced 'z', e.g. *zeven* (seven) and words beginning with 'f' were pronounced 'v', e.g. *vinger* (finger). The dialect was spoken slowly with vowels in one-syllable words spoken with a drawl, e.g. *maate* (meat), *coorn* (corn) and *caake* (cake). A characteristic of Forth and Bargy was that the stress shifted to the second syllable of two-syllable words, e.g. *dineare* (dinner), *weddeen* (wedding), etc. This feature can still be heard in Wexford speech to this day.

In 1652, two years after Cromwell departed Ireland, William Petty arrived, having been given the task of surveying the land that was to be confiscated and awarded to Cromwell's soldiers. In 1680, he was supplied with a series of reports on the baronies of Forth and Bargy. In the first it was stated that "they preserve their first language...the same form of apparel their predecessors first used...and seldom dispose of their children in marriage but unto natives, or such as will determine to reside in the barony."

According to an address given in Dublin in 1857 by Dr. Russell, the followers of Richard de Clare (Strongbow, 2nd Earl of Pembroke) and Robert FitzStephen were presumably recruited in the Pembrokeshire area. The mixed population of this area of South Wales consisted of not only Welsh, but also Anglo-Normans and a large number of Flemings who had settled in the area about fifty years earlier. In 1107 and again in 1113, the Low Countries suffered coastal flooding and many Flemings sought refuge in England. They were unpopular with the English peasantry and so King Henry I had them moved to one settlement around Haverfordwest in Pembrokeshire. More followed in 1138 as military adventurers in the reign of King Stephen (1135-54). These settlers brought not alone their form of the English language with a certain element of Flemish, but also their own customs and distinct dress.

Russell also referred to the community's form of siesta, or *enteete* in the local dialect, in summertime that they still adhered to: "they constantlie desist all works about ten o'clock ... reposing themselves and their ploughhorses until two of the clock, during which time all sorts of cattle are brought home from the field and kept enclosed." Colonel Richards, an old Cromwellian officer, then governor of Wexford, described the women of Forth: "in one particular they excel all their sex in this kingdom, viz. they so revere and honour the male sex, man, beast, and bird, that, to instance one particular only, if the master of the house be from home, his sonne, if any, or, if none, then his chief servant present, though but a poor plough-driver, or cowboy, shall have the first mess of broath, or cut of meat, before the mistress or her female guests, if she have any."

Russell added that the "youths and maidens of the new generation have grown ashamed of the ways of their elders". Even in 1788, when Charles Vallencey was compiling his short vocabulary, he had some difficulty finding anybody with a good knowledge of the old dialect. An old lady named Browne, also known as 'The Madam', and an elderly man named Dick Barry from Ballyconor near Kilrane, supplied Vallencey with the list of words. "Hardly one is now to be found in the entire district who uses it as a familiar tongue", added Dr. Russell in his 1857 address.

Russell agreed with Vallencey that "the Forth dialect is nothing more than the English of the invaders" and that the report to William Petty in 1680 described it as "old Saxon-English." Colonel Richards described it as "the very language brought over by FitzStephen". Richard Stanyhurst in his *Description of Ireland* was of the same opinion as Vallencey and Richards and added: "that in our daies they have so acquainted themselves with the Irish as they have made a mingle-mangle or gallimaufrere of both the languages, and have in such medley or checkerwise so crabbedlie jumbled them together, as commonlie the inhabitants of the meaner sort speak neither good English nor good Irish."

Similar to the Forth and Bargy dialect, Fingallian derived from Middle English and was spoken in the northern area of Fingal in north County Dublin. It too became extinct by the mid-19th century and both are believed to be the only dialects to have survived the original variety of English brought to Ireland 850 years ago.

These opening lines and translation are from probably the oldest example of the dialect to have survived, collected by Vallencey in the 18th century:

YOLA ZONG
Fade tell thee zo lournagh, co Joane, zo knaggee?
Th' weithest all curcagh, wafur, an conee.
Lidge w'ouse an a milagh, tis gaay an louthee:
Huck nigher; y'art scuddeen; fartoo zo hachee?

OLD SONG
What ails you so melancholy, quoth John, so cross?
You seem all snappish, uneasy, and fretful.
Lie with us on the clover, 'tis fair and sheltered:
Come nearer; you're rubbing your back; why so ill tempered?

Ros Tapestry: the Anglo-Norman tale told in thread

'Gothic Glory – Building of St. Mary's Church', embroidered at Bawnmore, New Ross.

THE ROS TAPESTRY is one of the largest series of tapestries in Europe. The 15 panels were embroidered by 150 volunteers over more than twenty years in a community initiative that began in 1998. The acclaimed tapestries depict the story of the development of the port town of Ros, later New Ross, consequent to the arrival in County Wexford of the Anglo-Normans in 1169.

The tapestries were inspired by the 70-metre-long Bayeux Tapestry in Normandy, which dates from the 1070s. This massive Norman Romanesque work illustrates some seventy scenes that tell the story of the events between 1064 and 1066 leading up to the Battle of Hastings in which the Norman-French decisively defeated the Anglo-Saxons.

Richard de Clare (Strongbow), Earl of Pembroke, arrived at Passage in 1170 as part of the Anglo-Norman occupation and assumed control of Leinster and the Norse-Gaelic settlements of Waterford, Wexford and Dublin in rapid succession. He had been promised the hand of Diarmait's daughter Aoife in marriage and on the day after taking Waterford, Strongbow and Aoife of Leinster married in Waterford's Christ Church Cathedral.

When Strongbow died six years later leaving no adult heir, the Crown assumed control of his lands in Wales and Ireland. His young daughter Isabel was a ward of the Crown and this meant that the reigning monarch had the right to choose her husband. William Marshal, also known as Guillaume Le Marechal, was born in Caversham near Reading to John FitzGilbert the Marshal, who had been the royal marshal to King Henry I. William trained as a knight in Normandy, where he was knighted in 1166. While serving in the court of King Henry II, he was promised the hand and estates of Isabel de Clare, Countess of Pembroke and daughter of Strongbow.

In 1189, the 43-year-old landless knight Marshal married 17-year-old Isabel in London, thereby acquiring large estates in England, Wales, Normandy and Ireland, including most of counties Wexford, Carlow and Kilkenny. William and Isabel established Kilkenny, Carlow and Ferns castles as well as Tintern Abbey. Strongbow is believed to have had a castle at Old Ross but William and Isabel shifted the centre of the demesne and borough to a more strategic location on the River Barrow. Developed between 1192 and 1207, New Ross was one of the first Anglo-Norman towns in Ireland and

The ruin of the 800-year-old St. Mary's Church in New Ross, attributed to William Marshal and Isabel de Clare, whose heart is reputed to be buried within its walls. (photo: Des Kiely)

replaced the old Gaelic settlement of Ros. A fine bridge was built across the Barrow and a new town grew up around it that became known as *Pons Novus* (New Bridge) or *Ros Ponte* and subsequently New Ross.

Embroiderers at work on one of the panels.
(photo courtesy Ros Tapestry)

The very powerful and wealthy couple lived for most of the time in Kilkenny Castle and through the port of New Ross they traded with their lands in Wales and beyond. They commissioned the construction of Hook Lighthouse to protect the entrance from the sea to the Barrow, serving New Ross and Carlow and the Nore to Kilkenny. William and Isabel were happily married for 30 years and had five sons and five daughters.

It is believed that they founded St. Mary's Church in New Ross, built on the ruins of the 6th century monastery of St. Abban. It had a commanding view over the Barrow and was completed in 1210. The remains of the church, one of the first Gothic churches built in Ireland, are the town's only surviving built evidence linked to the Marshal family. Isabel died 800 years ago in 1220 and a small tomb within the ancient walls is believed to contain her heart. It bears the legend *Isabel: Laegn* (Isabel of Leinster). A section of the medieval structure was demolished in about 1812, when the Church of Ireland erected a new church on the site. Reverend Paul Mooney, a former Catholic priest, was appointed rector of St. Mary's in 1998. He conceived the idea of having a series of tapestries, depicting the Anglo-Norman history of the area, produced and displayed in his church. Rev. Mooney consulted with Alexis Bernstorff, a local art historian

William Marshal, a detail from the marriage tapestry – embroidered in Bunclody House.

Detail from the panel depicting the marriage of William Marshal and Isabel de Clare.

and specialist in tapestry and fabric restoration. His mother, Ann Griffin-Bernstorff, a professional artist, was commissioned to produce the illustrations from which the panels have been embroidered. Ann also acted as historian for the project. The first tapestry panel, depicting Hook Lighthouse, was made by a group of volunteer stitchers working in the parish hall in Poulfour, Fethard-on-Sea, starting in 2000 and completing the work three years later. Alexis Bernstorff supervised the training of the stitchers and the production of all 15 panels. They were embroidered by 150 volunteers at various locations throughout County Wexford, some in private houses, and one was produced in Kilkenny – a great example of community spirit and creativity on a grand scale. Each panel measures approximately 1.8 x 1.2m (6 by 4 feet) and tells the story of the arrival of the Anglo-Normans and the consequent development of the dynamic port town of Ros.

The embroiderers describe the style of stitching that they employed as 'needle painting' as they indicate shape, volume and movement in the work. They first traced the original illustration on clear acetate, which was then placed on a large lightbox. The linen was pinned over the acetate and, with the lights switched on, the drawing was traced with pencil as the image projected through. The linen was then ready to be stretched onto the loom and then the stitching began. With up to four people at a time working on the loom, each panel took between 3 and 8 years to complete.

In 2007, New Ross celebrated its 800th anniversary and the panel *William Marshal – The Flower of Chivalry*, completed in September 2007, was launched at the Ros 800 Expo. As the project progressed it became obvious that the 15 panels were going to be too large to display in St. Mary's Church. It was decided to hang all the embroideries in a permanent exhibition elsewhere in the town and so the Ros Tapestry Exhibition Centre was opened on the quay in 2009. The centre has a charitable status and is dependent on the financial support of its many supporters, friends, sponsors and patrons. The exhibition is open to the public all year round. You can see all the tapestries and read the full story behind each at www.rostapestry.ie

These are the fifteen panels that make up the exhibition:

THE CELTS – AN ISLAND FASTNESS
– embroidered in Crossabeg and Johnstown Castle

THE ABDUCTION OF DERVOGILLA
– embroidered near Ferns

ARROGANT TRESPASS – NORMANS LANDING AT BANNOW
– embroidered at Duncannon Fort

'The Abduction of Dervogilla' – a detail from the panel embroidered near Ferns.

'William Marshal - the Flower of Chivalry' – embroidered in Crossabeg and Oylegate.

THE SIEGE OF WEXFORD
– embroidered in the National Heritage Park and Johnstown Castle

BATTLES IN THE KINGDOM OF OSSORY
– embroidered at Rothe House, Kilkenny

THE MARRIAGE OF ISABEL DE CLARE AND WILLIAM MARSHAL
– embroidered in the library of Bunclody House

WILLIAM MARSHAL – THE FLOWER OF CHIVALRY
– embroidered at private homes in Crossabeg and Oylegate

EX VOTO TINTERN ABBEY - MARSHAL'S STORMY CROSSING
– embroidered at the Parish Hall in Poulfour, Fethard-on-Sea

HUNT IN THE FOREST OF ROS
– embroidered in Clonroche

GOTHIC GLORY – BUILDING OF ST. MARY'S CHURCH
– embroidered at Bawnmore, New Ross

EVENING – THE LIGHTHOUSE AT HOOK HEAD
– embroidered at the Parish Hall in Poulfour, Fethard-on-Sea

THE THRIVING PORT OF ROS
– embroidered in Clonroche

'Normans Landing at Bannow' – detail from the panel embroidered at Duncannon Fort.

THE WALLING OF ROS – SIXTEEN GUILDS PROTECT THEIR TOWN
– embroidered in New Ross

EXCHANGE – THE IRISH AND NORMANS MINGLE AT THE FAIR
– embroidered in New Ross

THE SHEAF OF CORN – THE DISTAFF DESCENT
– embroidered at Bawnmore, New Ross

(All tapestries photographed by Des Kiely and Nadia Michnik)

'The Siege of Wexford' – from the panel embroidered in the National Heritage Park and Johnstown Castle.

Bibliography

Books

Blake Knox, David, *Suddenly, While Abroad* (Dublin, 2012)

Borrow, George, *Celebrated Trials* (London, 1825)

Brady, Karl, *Warships, U-Boats & Liners* (Dublin, 2012)

Carroll, Katherine, *The Energy of Place - The Magic of Yoletown Farm* (Wexford, 2017)

Corish, Patrick, *The Irish Martyrs and Irish History, Archivium Hibernicum* (Dublin, 1993)

De Abreu, Juan, *History of the Discovery and Conquest of the Canary Islands* (Dublin, 1767)

Fenton, Laurence, *Frederick Douglass in Ireland* (Cork, 2014)

Fullarton, Archibald and Co., *Parliamentary Gazetteer of Ireland* (Glasgow, 1846)

Griffiths, George, *Chronicles of the County Wexford* (Enniscorthy, 1890)

Hore, Philip Herbert, *History of the Town and County of Wexford* (London, 1900-11)

Lewis, Samuel, *A Topographical Dictionary of Ireland* (London, 1837)

McNamara, Dr Conor, *The Easter Rebellion 1916* (Cork, 2015)

Molony, Senan, *The Irish Aboard Titanic* (Cork, 2000)

Mooney, Tom and Eustace, Stephen, *Battlefield* (Enniscorthy, 1998)

Poole, Jacob, *Old Dialect in the Baronies of Forth and Bargy* (London, 1867)

Roche, Richard, *Tales of the Wexford Coast* (Enniscorthy, 1993)

Shine, Potterton, Mandal, McLoughlin (Ed.), *Carrick, County Wexford* (Dublin, 2019)

Snoek, Michael, *Master of the Forge* (Wexford, 2009)

Newspapers

Bray People

County Echo, Wales

Enniscorthy Guardian

Gorey Guardian

Irish Press

Irish Times

New Ross Standard

Wexford Free Press

Wexford Herald

Wexford Independent

Wexford People

Other sources

Buildings of Ireland

Bureau of Military History, Dublin

History Ireland

Irish Heritage Trust

Irish Military Archives

JSTOR Digital Library

National Library of Ireland

National Museum of Ireland

RTÉ Archives

Wexford County Library